Governors State University
Library
Hours:
Monday thru Thursday 8:30 to 10:30
Friday and Saturday 8:30 to 5:00
Sunday 1:00 to 5:00 (Fall and Winter Trimester Only)

DEMCO

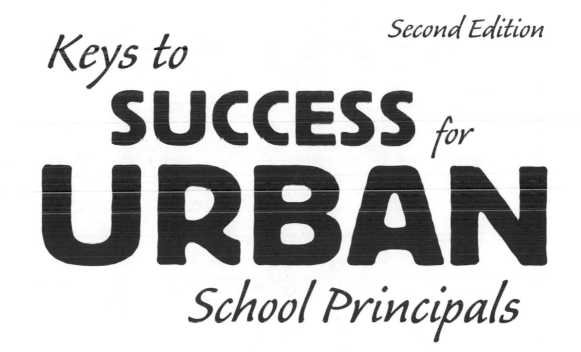

Second Edition

Keys to

SUCCESS for

URBAN

School Principals

To my good friend and supporter Elaine Melmed,
who encouraged me to begin this project
and remained my ally over the years.
Elaine continues to remind me that
"not failure, but low aim, is sin."

Second Edition

Keys to SUCCESS for URBAN School Principals

Gwendolyn J. Cooke

CORWIN PRESS
A SAGE Publications Company
Thousand Oaks, CA 91320

For information:

Corwin Press
A Sage Publications Company
2455 Teller Road
Thousand Oaks, California 91320
www.corwinpress.com

Sage Publications Ltd.
1 Oliver's Yard
55 City Road
London EC1Y 1SP
United Kingdom

Sage Publications India Pvt. Ltd.
B-42, Panchsheel Enclave
Post Box 4109
New Delhi 110 017 India

Printed in the United States of America.

Library of Congress Cataloging-in-Publication Data

Cooke, Gwendolyn J.
Keys to success for urban school principals / Gwendolyn J. Cooke. — 2nd ed.
    p. cm.
Includes bibliographical references and index.
ISBN 1-4129-4092-3 or 978-1-412940-92-4 (cloth)
ISBN 1-4129-4093-1 or 978-1-412940-93-1 (pbk.)
  1. School principals—United States. 2. Education, Urban—United States. I. Title.

LB2831.92.C67 2007
371.2′0120973—dc22   2006017031

This book is printed on acid-free paper.

06 07 08 09 10 11 9 8 7 6 5 4 3 2 1

Acquisitions Editor:	Cathy Hernandez
Editorial Assistant:	Charline Wu
Production Editor:	Diane S. Foster
Copy Editor:	Diana Breti
Typesetter:	C&M Digitals (P) Ltd.
Proofreader:	Kevin Gleason
Indexer:	Molly Hall
Cover Designer:	Monique Hahn

Contents

Preface

When I worked for the National Association of Secondary School Principals, I worked closely with a group of practicing urban principals and assistant principals who had as one of their challenges the goal of "identifying solutions to the challenges facing urban secondary school administrators." Over the years, these principals kept returning to the need for a resource document that experienced and neophyte urban principals could use to "take charge" humanistically of a large complex organization. Many of these principals with whom I worked in the late 1990s reflected about their work and are responsible for the key "C's"—control, caring, change, charisma, communication, curriculum, and courage—that identify the chapters in this book. These dedicated men and women, residing in cities whose populations exceeded 200,000, advocated for policies and publications that could be used by them and their elementary school peers. They repeatedly acknowledged the need for systemic reform, but they also felt that a resource document that spoke to the conditions of urban schools and used the language with which urban school administrations were conversant would be picked up by school administrators and used. They acknowledged the utility of existing generic documents on the principalship, change, and reform, but appealed for their own "little red book," their own manual for excellence, their own Bible, their own Torah! This book is an answer to their call.

When I first assumed a principalship at an elementary urban school, I inherited an excellent teaching and support staff but no organized set of documents to guide my work. There was no student handbook. There was no faculty and staff handbook. There was no parent and community handbook. There was no school improvement action plan even though there were school district goals and objectives for which each school was held accountable. There was no organized parent, student, and teacher association. The school records, both student and staff records, were not organized. I made a pledge to myself that when I left that elementary school, the principal following me would not be greeted with the same challenges I was. When I left the school seven months later, the new principal had nothing but accolades for me. The transition conference, buttressed by the documents I gave to the new principal, prepared the new principal for the duties he was about to assume.

The second principalship I assumed in the same school district was more difficult than the first for several reasons. The staff I inherited was not as competent, and it was three times larger than the one I left behind. The student body was five times larger. Record keeping and standard documents, again, were either nonexistent or had not been revised, with faculty and staff input, in eight years. Consequently, the documents did not comply with district, state, and federal guidelines.

I reflected on my second experience and decided to conduct a survey of newly appointed principals in the school district to determine their experiences. To my surprise, less than 20% of the "newly" appointed principals found documents (or were given documents by the outgoing principal) that would facilitate the effective operation of the school.

These three demonstrable reasons coupled with the biased media coverage (some because of proximity) and the uneven academic achievement of urban students, as reported in national achievement data, support the need for urban school principals to have their own "little red book" to inform their instructional and administrative practice. I offer it in the memory of those school administrators who have lost their lives in the line of duty. Unfortunately, in too many of the schools where life has been lost, students felt alienated and they struck out at people nearest them—their peers, their teachers, their guidance counselors, school security, and their principals and assistant principals. There are no guarantees about what will work in any school. Ten years as a principal in two urban schools taught me much. One thing I know is that it is possible to transform a school climate from one of indifference and permissiveness to one of control, communicating, and caring. During my first two years as a principal in the large secondary school (1,400 students), I took loaded guns, knives, metal pipes, metal chains, broken bottles, and other objects used as weapons from angry, violent students. Using the strategies in this book, changed the academic, organizational, social-emotional, and physical climates in the school. The number of student referrals, out-of-school suspensions, and expulsions plummeted. Students' academic achievement increased. Parent and community involvement increased. Funding increased because of the grant writing of staff, parents, and partners. After three years, the school received the Greater Baltimore Committee's (Chamber of Commerce) Outstanding Middle School of the Year Award. The award was based on these criteria: student academic achievement; student and staff attendance; student discipline records; school climate; and parent, business, and community involvement.

Effective principals are those who have made a commitment to improve their ability to influence and to motivate others. In being expressive and supportive, they make room for their own humanness, continuing to learn and to grow along with the people they work with. They do not always do things perfectly, but they do things. They do not always say profound things, but they say something. They can laugh and be serious; they can be inconsistent and still know how to follow through on important priorities. They can be firm and, at times, flexible. They are able to be effective and realistic.

I would advise school leaders to never let the freedom and challenge to grow become an obligation to be perfect. There is no such thing as a perfect principal. I have "walked in your moccasins," and I know about the challenges you face. What I remember most about the principalship, however, are the hugs and verbal thanks from students and their extended families; the teacher notes and public pronouncements that working with me had contributed to significant professional and personal growth; the active recruitment of my staff by my principal colleagues and some central offices; working with fellow principals who were willing to coach and mentor me during challenging times; and three superintendents (Dr. Roland Patterson, Dr. John Crew, Mrs. Alice Pinderhughes) who understood what it meant to let "a thousand flowers bloom." I was allowed to lead with grace and dignity. I wish you grace, and I wish you dignity as you lead, lifting you as you climb!

Acknowledgments

From 1995 through February, 2000, urban secondary school principals serving on the National Association of Secondary School Principals' Urban Schools Committee provided support and motivation for me to write this book. The principals validated my research and experiences by brainstorming the initial "C's" developed in this book. The principals also provided suggestions, reviewed various drafts of the compendium of strategies (initiating, stabilizing, sustaining), and took wagers on who would publish my manuscript and how much it would cost!

Special thanks to two NASSP board members who supported the efforts to keep urban school issues on the association's priority list: J. Patrick Mahon of Norcross, GA, and John Osteen of Norfolk, VA; and to the urban school principals with whom I worked most closely: Linda B. Transou, Cozette M. Buckney, Michael E. Anderson, Thomas F. Balistreri, John L. Mancini, Eugene Young, III, Jerome C. Winegar, Patricia A. Batiste-Brown, Michael W. Evans, Sr., Gary L. Huskey, Kathy L. Deniro, and Audrey J. Donaldson. Kudos and thanks to each of you.

I am greatly indebted to the editors at Corwin Press who helped give birth to the second edition of this book. Without your thoughtful guidance, the completion of this book would have been prolonged. Thanks for your editorial assistance and friendship.

PUBLISHER'S ACKNOWLEDGMENTS

Corwin Press gratefully acknowledges the contributions of the following reviewers:

Rosalind Pijeaux Hale
Professor of Education
Xavier University of Louisiana, New Orleans, LA

Karen Janney
Principal
Montgomery High School, San Diego, CA

Barbara Rudiak
Principal
Phillips Elementary School, Pittsburgh, PA

Anne Smith
Education Research Analyst
Office of Special Education Programs
U.S. Department of Education, Washington, DC

Patricia Long Tucker
Assistant Superintendent
District of Columbia Public Schools, Washington, DC

Doreatha White
Principal
Dreamkeepers Academy
J. J. Roberts Elementary, Norfolk, VA

About the Author

 Prior to being named Deputy Superintendent of Kansas City, MO School District, **Dr. Gwendolyn J. Cooke** worked in senior level positions in these urban districts: Warrensville Heights, OH; Cincinnati, OH; Savannah, GA; and Baltimore, MD. For a decade, Dr. Cooke directed programs and services for urban and rural schools at the National Association of Secondary School Principals (NASSP). Having attained the status of trainer of trainers, Dr. Cooke is certified to train others in the use of many of NASSP's professional development programs for school leaders. Her areas of expertise include leadership development of school administrators, gifted and talented education, standards-based school reform, multicultural education, NCLB regulations, parent and community involvement, and educating special education and economically disadvantaged children. The year 2006 marks Dr. Cooke's 37th year as an educator in schools and universities delivering quality services to learners.

Introduction

What are the forces that are changing the nature of the principalship generally, and the urban principalship specifically? Where are they coming from? Are they new and different from the forces that shaped the schools of yesterday? How are they affecting schools?

Consider this list of forces that help shape the urban principal's behaviors; they may be positive or negative, depending on where you sit.

- Teachers are becoming teacher-leaders.
- Parents are more vocal and action-oriented advocates.
- Student bodies are more diverse with a variety of needs.
- The social and technological contexts of schools are more complex.
- State and federal mandates are setting priorities. (Goldring & Rallis, 2000)

As an urban school principal for ten years, my behavior was affected by each of these forces along with others. I considered each of them positive forces because implicit in each is the call for collaboration with various stakeholders, and because they required that I be creative and open to new ideas and ways of thinking.

Recent research by the Pew Charitable Trusts and conversations by college professors in schools of education across the country are addressing the need for focused thinking, systemic approaches, and acknowledgment that urban schools are "different" and therefore require "different" solutions to increasing their productiveness.

In collaboration with *Education Week*, the Pew Charitable Trusts published two reports focusing on urban schools titled "Quality Counts: The Urban Challenge Report" ("Quality Counts," 1998). Each report highlights the special characteristics of urban districts and the demands they place on urban school administrators. In the 1998 report, nine barriers to urban schools' success are cited: crippling politics, aging infrastructure, dense bureaucracy, poverty, violence, lack of money, the teaching challenge, a rapid turnover in administrators, and school climate. The reports are not limited, however, to the problems urban schools face. Fifteen approaches that experienced success are showcased and offered as models for school districts that are committed to increasing urban students' academic achievement.

A faculty and staff study group at four schools of education within the University of California system defined the challenges faced by urban school leaders somewhat differently. Their observations focus specifically on the students' behaviors, attitudes, and skill levels, students' parents' backgrounds, institutional practices of schools, the quality of the teaching force, and the nature of the communities in which the students live (Deans of School of Education, 1999).

For this group of scholars, students' value of schooling colors and is responsible for their inconsistent engagement in academic and cocurricular activities. When one couples this ambivalance with the parents' modest levels of schooling (lack of a high school diploma) or differences in cultural background (parents who come from countries with different school traditions), the challenge is magnified. The problem becomes even larger when the students are retained at a given grade level because they cannot perform at their age and grade level.

Dissatisfied with the school district's performance with their children, urban parents and district and state officials exert pressure, and laws are enacted to improve urban students' performance. Schools adopt "no pass, no play" and "no social promotion" policies that result in a contradiction: The very students identified as needing help are affected by the policies that exclude them from engagement in transferable foundation learning experiences. The new policies also lead to much faculty, staff, and administrative stress.

Language issues are complex in urban schools. Students come from many different language groups, and some come to school without Standard English. Newcomers' programs abound in urban centers. According to the study group, the racial and ethnic diversity of urban schools creates another set of distinctive issues, sometimes reflected in conflicts among students, sometimes in misunderstandings between faculty and students or between educators and parents.

The California scholars point out as well that school districts' institutional practices often operate to limit and constrain educational opportunities for urban students rather than to expand and enrich them. One example is school districts' policies that outline admissions to honors courses and SAT preparation courses. Usually, successful completion of a prerequisite course and a set score on a standardized test are required for enrollment and/or placement.

Urban students may suffer more than others from being in anonymous settings where no one knows them well. It is common for urban students to be in classes with 30 or more students or in classes where 20% of the students have special needs that are not being addressed appropriately. Resources in urban schools and districts often seem to be stretched thin. Couple this with students residing in neighborhoods that are turbulent and the difficulty students must experience with deciding whom to trust, and one has a unique challenge.

In urban school districts, the teaching force is often inexperienced and untrained, hired with emergency credentials or training in special, short programs. Teacher training programs often fail to prepare teachers for the particular characteristics of urban schools. This lack of preparation is sometimes because the courses are often taught by white male professors whose knowledge of urban schools, at-risk students, and minority cultures comes from secondary sources. In addition, teachers' beliefs about their own efficacy have significant implications for the quality of education and the ultimate achievement of urban students.

A basic prerequisite to learning in school is an openness on the part of the student to accept the teacher as a credible source. For this to occur, the student should feel that the teacher is significant to him or her in a positive way. Negative attitudes and stereotypes on the part of the teacher may destroy this tenuous, crucial bond, or prevent it from ever developing, thereby creating student resistance to the teacher both personally and educationally (Payne, 1998, p. 6).

Negative teacher attitudes that cause or can be interpreted as withdrawal or rejection have an effect on students' sense of efficacy, productivity, performance, and involvement in school. Teacher-student connection is meaningful because teachers are in control of many variables that create motivation and achievement, such as task, content, social organization, activity choice, and material resources. *When teachers do not believe they control the conditions under which students learn, and when they hold negative attitudes and stereotypes about the students they teach, they do not bond with the students and they do not teach them well.*

A teacher's belief that *he or she can teach* is a powerful factor. If a teacher strongly believes that *students can learn* and that *he or she can teach*, the teacher is less likely to engage in negative instructional practices and behaviors. Teachers with a high sense of personal efficacy are more confident and at ease in their classrooms, and they demonstrate more positive communication with their students (e.g., praising, smiling). They are also better classroom managers, less defensive, and more accepting of student disagreement and challenges; they produce greater student achievement as a result.

Effective teachers are those who believe that ability is not static or limited to the select, but that all students are capable of learning. Consequently, they communicate this to students in as many ways as possible, and the significant teacher-student relationship that evolves *positively* influences motivation. This has great bearing on economically poor students, for whom the factors influencing motivation are frequently destroyed or in opposition to the purposes of schooling.

Several deleterious conditions exist that are exacerbated by negative teacher attitudes and stereotypes. These conditions have been firmly established in the research literature and include lower track-level placement of minority students; lowered expectations and reduced opportunities; and differences between school personnel and students in language, lifestyles, values, personal preferences, cognitive and social styles, and occupational aspirations. Individually or in combination, these factors can create problematic relationships between teachers and urban minority students. As a result, frequent discipline problems deprive these students of meaningful instruction. (The students are removed from school and therefore are not present for instruction.) However, to be effective while maintaining their own sense of efficacy, teachers must gain the students' trust and become significant to them despite these conditions.

An understanding of and attention to teacher efficacy research is imperative for urban school leaders committed to urban school reform that results in increased student academic achievement.

Table 0.1 summarizes the research about urban schools' challenges highlighted in this Introduction. Because of the way the media telescopes these challenges and the way members of the community seem to internalize these challenges and point to the school for resolution, Table 0.1 is offered to underscore to urban school administrators that it is *not* their responsibility to resolve *all problems confronting urban schools.* It is easy to fall into the trap of being the "great white hope" who has solutions for all

Table 0.1   Common Problems Faced by Urban School Principals

Common Problems/ Barriers	Families and the Community	School Board	District Office	School Principal and Staff
Crippling politics	X	X		
Aging infrastructure	X	X	X	
Poverty	X	X	X	X
Community violence	X	X		
Lack of money	X	X		
Racial and cultural issues	X	X	X	X
NonEnglish language learners	X	X	X	X
Rapid turnover of school administrators		X	X	X
Quality of the teaching force		X	X	X
Teacher beliefs				X
School climate				X
Student retention				X
Student poor attendance				X
Criteria for student admission to ACT/ SAT classes				X
Criteria for student enrollment in Honors classes				X
Criteria for student participation in cocurricular activitie				X
Over-identification of Special Education students				X

school barriers and challenges. The responsibility for urban schools is a *shared responsibility.* Acknowledgment of this fact does not constitute an attempt to shirk accountability for addressing legitimate school problems. Resolution of some problems is not possible without those problems being embraced by the larger community. Other problem resolutions are those that fall within the school or school district's domain.

Although this book provides seven strategies—the seven C's—for addressing urban school issues, these strategies are not offered as a panacea. However, staff at the school, district, and school board level can and must accept the leadership responsibility for some of the problems. The Reflective Practice Exercises in Chapters 1 to 6 contain specific practices— initiating, stabilizing, and sustaining—that can be used with teachers and students to implement positive changes. For example, the barriers of students' alienating attitudes and behaviors may be addressed by using the Exercises in Chapters 1, 2, and 5.

NO CHILD LEFT BEHIND ◼

The No Child Left Behind Act (NCLB), signed into law in January, 2002, has become a symbol of all things good and bad in education. The language of NCLB speaks to the sweeping authority intended by its passage:

> The purpose of this title is to ensure that all children have a fair, equal, and significant opportunity to obtain a high-quality education and reach, at a minimum, proficiency on challenging state academic achievement standards and state academic assessments. (McColl, 2005)

To accomplish this, NCLB sets extensive requirements for states, including establishing an accountability system, staffing schools with high quality professionals, and making unique provisions for parent involvement.

NCLB requires that supplemental educational services—free tutoring programs—primarily are offered to students who qualify for free or reduced-price lunches if their schools have failed for three years to make adequate yearly progress (AYP). Making AYP means a school has met state academic standards in reading and mathematics by 2014.

School districts are *required* to make parents aware of this opportunity for extra academic help for their children. Parents can choose from lists of providers approved by their states.

Districts must reserve 20% of the federal Title I money they receive to pay for these tutoring services and for transportation for students who choose to change schools under another provision of the law.

NCLB was welcomed by most urban school leaders because of its accountability provisions for disaggregating data by subgroups of students, and for the requirement of testing 95% of the student body. Closing the achievement gap is of paramount importance to urban school principals, and the federal law puts the issue front and center. Too often, urban school leaders have felt that critics have implied that students from low-income families and students of color simply cannot be expected to achieve at high levels.

Although welcomed, other NCLB provisions are more problematic, such as the mandate that by the end of the 2005–2006 school year a "highly qualified" teacher must be in every classroom in which a core subject is taught. For many urban school districts, it is very difficult to find highly qualified teachers for every core subject. Moreover, frequently secondary teachers teach more than one subject because of the lack of qualified candidates. Veteran teachers also face hurdles because of changes in certification over the years. To acknowledge their years of classroom experience fairly, many veteran teachers have been grandfathered into state certification systems.

Other "highly qualified teacher" challenges include, but are not limited to, these:

- Class size reduction requirements in effect for grades K–3
- Annual attrition rates of 5% or more
- Some local boards disagreeing with the law and failing to comply with it
- Most or all of middle schools in a district having been labeled as needing improvement/low performing resulting in the lack of parents' "transfer choices"

The NCLB Act has resulted in these *positive changes:*

- Staff development plans for instructing teachers how to better assist special populations of students
- Schedules that focus more time on core subject areas and allow flexible grouping
- Practices to provide instruction at individualized levels
- Creative tutoring schedules that provide extra assistance to individual students.
- Changes in assessment practices that enable educators to use data to make better instructional decisions (Standerfer, 2005)

NCLB has also had unintended consequences in school practices:

- Students attending school on standardized test days even when they are ill simply to meet the "95% tested" requirement in all subgroups
- Students taking remedial review courses to prepare for state exams
- Special education students taking state assessments that are known to be above the students' level of functioning
- Pay for performance plans that have high quality teachers questioning whether they are willing to teach special education or English language learner students (Standerfer, 2005)

Challenges to NCLB continue as of this writing. The National Education Association, several NEA affiliates, and nine school districts filed a lawsuit claiming that NCLB was an unfunded mandate. The U.S. Department of Education continues to issue guidance documents, letters to chief state school officers and state officials, and formal regulations to clarify key issues, including public school choice requirements, standards and assessments, the definition of a highly qualified teacher, the inclusion of students with significant cognitive disabilities, and several aspects of the accountability model.

The U.S. Department of Education announced that it would allow up to 10 states to implement a growth model pilot program to measure student progress. Currently, NCLB uses an improvement model, which tracks proficiency by comparing student cohort groups. A growth model would measure progress by tracking individual students' achievement from year to year.

Although the face NCLB wears may be modified, the law is here to stay. Moreover, it is highly unlikely that the disaggregating of data by ethnicity, economic status (free/reduced lunch eligibility), program status (ESL, special education) and grade level will be changed. Thus, urban school principals should embrace the changes and lead their faculties and staff to improved student achievement along with other outcomes that nurture and develop students for success at whatever next level awaits them.

OVERVIEW OF CHAPTERS AND HOW TO USE THIS BOOK

Keys to Success for Urban School Principals is presented in seven chapters. Each chapter opens with a scenario for the reader's consideration. Each scenario focuses on a facet of the urban school principalship: control, caring, change, charisma, communication, curriculum, and courage. The text that follows combines research and practical strategies for effectively leading an urban school.

"Unlocking" strategies appear throughout each chapter and provide a vantage point from which readers can pause and think about what they have just read and how it applies to their experience. Reflective Practice Exercises appear at the end of each chapter for use with input from your colleagues and staff or as part of small group discussions or planning meetings. The exercises are designed to refine your leadership practice. You might even want to start your exploration of this book by looking at the exercises first and then reading through the chapter text.

Control: Managing the School Community is addressed in Chapter 1. Management of an urban school cannot be left to chance. Instead, national standards and excellence theory must be employed by the urban school principal to unlock his or her own efficacy. Continual self-assessment and acting on the results of such assessments can be the key to a principal's attainment of his or her personal and professional objectives.

The underlying theme of the first chapter is that principals gain and maintain control by seeking and building consensus from all the school's stakeholders.

Caring: Addressing the Affective Domain of Leadership Success is the central theme of Chapter 2. Urban schools can be sanctuaries that nurture students' intellects and spirits. The affective aspect of leadership is the heart and soul of leadership. Listening to and respecting students' voice and experience must be part of any discussion about the nature of schooling. The school climate as defined actively by adults can either invite students to learn, grow, and explore or it can do just the opposite—inhibit or stifle learning and the desire to learn. Recognizing that not all students or students' families are the same, nor do they need to be, is a key component of caring in an urban school.

Managing by Walking Around (MBWA) is just one method described in Chapter 2 that a principal can use to evidence caring while effectively managing staff and students.

Change: Leading in a New Direction is Chapter 3's focus. Change is a scary prospect for most of us. Change is not an outcome but a process. The forces of change have fundamentally altered the nature of contemporary principalship, particularly in the urban school. An effective school leader must assertively and intentionally address conflict and use it to power constructive change.

Chapter 3 reviews existing literature related to organizational change and how schools can use these theories. Study circles are recommended as one effective strategy to use prior to implementing a major change. It is important to remember that change takes time and patience.

Charisma: Leading With Personality is Chapter 4. The chapter acknowledges how a principal is expected to be all things to all people. Charisma can often be the key to managing these disparate expectations. While the definition of charisma varies, its utility is unquestioned. Determining how to cultivate your own charismatic potential is the subject of this chapter.

Communication: Sharing Vision and Commitment for Success is the topic of Chapter 5. The chapter is devoted to a discussion of the importance of effective oral and written communication. A principal's oral communication skills are assessed by all stakeholders in a variety of settings, including one-on-one, small groups, large groups, and large group meetings, as well as when the principal performs his or her regular duties.

Failure to communicate with key stakeholders (parents, students, partners) will derail all initiatives that could increase student achievement. Collegial conversations can elevate professionalism in the school. Such conversations, however, require courage and risk taking, components of leadership discussed in Chapter 7.

Curriculum: The Tool for Instructional Leadership constitutes Chapter 6, which explores the power of curriculum and strategies for harnessing that power. Curriculum leadership is the essence of instructional leadership. The urban school principal needs to be conversant in curriculum trends and the nature and role national organizations play in promulgating core content subject areas. Internet sites are offered so leaders may connect to up-to-date resources and other leaders.

The null and hidden curriculums result in negative student attitudes and school outcomes that require an inordinate amount of the principal's time. An awareness of their destructiveness should prompt urban principals to make curriculum an ongoing priority.

Courage: Risk Taking and Responsibility is Chapter 7, which examines how a leader's willingness to take risks can affect his or her success as a leader. Calculated risk is an essential component of leadership. Embracing conflict takes courage. Principals should not avoid conflict but rather use it to power change and advance student achievement. To find and implement solutions to a school's most perplexing problems, the urban school principal must have the courage to employ responsible risk taking.

This book may be used for any number of purposes.

Candidates in educational leadership training programs, educators participating in district "new" administrators' programs, as well as experienced, practicing administrators engaged in professional development may benefit from this book. As regards educational leadership training programs, the Reflective Practice Exercises can easily be used as module activities in internship programs that prepare urban school leaders.

As "new" urban school administrators first take on the sometimes overwhelming task of running a school, they will find the seven C's useful in their work. They will also discover that the framework can help them keep the different aspects of their role in perspective, to see the many and immediate demands placed on them in the service of the school's instructional mission.

As *experienced administrators* seek to improve their practice, they will discover that the C's can guide their efforts. Through self-assessment, goal setting, and self-directed professional inquiry, administrators can discover where their greatest needs lie and can plan accordingly.

INTERSTATE SCHOOL LEADERS LICENSURE CONSORTIUM (ISLLC) STANDARDS FOR SCHOOL LEADERSHIP

Since the first edition of this book was published, the Interstate School Leaders Licensure Consortium (ISLLC) Standards for School Leadership have been adopted for use by state departments and school districts throughout the country (Council of Chief State School Officers, 1996). The standards define and guide the practice of school leaders.

The ISLLC Standards

Standard 1

A school administrator is an educational leader who promotes the success of all students by facilitating the development, articulation, implementation, and stewardship of a vision of learning that is shared and supported by the school community.

Standard 2

A school administrator is an educational leader who promotes the success of all students by advocating, nurturing, and sustaining a school culture and instructional program conducive to student learning and staff professional growth.

Standard 3

A school administrator is an educational leader who promotes the success of all students by ensuring management of the organization, operations, and resources for a safe, efficient, and effective learning environment.

Standard 4

A school administrator is an educational leader who promotes the success of all students by collaborating with families and community members, responding to diverse community interests and needs, and mobilizing community resources.

(Continued)

■ ESTABLISHING CONTROL

You want to win, and as the principal you feel that your position of authority puts you in control. But it is important to recognize that you can never hold all the cards. You cannot control others; at best, you influence them. You do not even motivate others; you establish a context that invites their own motivation. Your only "control" is over the environment you provide that makes winning probable. You can control only your own performance—the frequency, quality, timing, and responsiveness of your efforts—and even that is in question on Monday mornings.

■ TIME MANAGEMENT

Effective instructional leaders must *manage time* well. There is no right or wrong way to manage time, but there are more effective and less effective ways to do it. Maintaining a daily log of how much time you spend on particular activities is fundamental to managing your time more effectively. Consider these strategies:

1. Set aside time each day to review and prioritize demands on your time.

2. Identify a small chunk of a difficult task, then deal with it right away.

3. Think through your day while making your way to work.

4. Always delegate tasks that are not time-effective for you to do.

5. Split your working day into chunks of 30 minutes each.

6. Keep a Time Diary in intervals of 15 minutes for three consecutive days. Stop every hour and catch up on the diary entries. Do not trust your memory. The only way for you to make better use of your time is to *analyze* how you use it now—do this on the fourth day—and then to consider ways in which you can reallocate it in a more effective way. When analyzing how you use time, consider using these criteria: urgent and important, important and not urgent, not important and urgent, not important and not urgent.

Below are some additional thoughts about time:

Deadlines: Deadlines can aid in overcoming indecision and procrastination.

Efficient vs. Effective: Efficient means doing things right. Effective means doing the right thing.

Scheduling: Scheduled events are more likely to happen than unscheduled events.

Murphy's Laws: (1) Nothing is as simple as it seems. (2) Everything takes longer than you think. (3) If anything can go wrong, it will.

Parkinson's Law: Work expands to fill the time available for its accomplishment.

Here are representative "time wasters" I experienced as a beginning urban school principal: drop-in visitors, crisis situations (discipline, custodial, aging infrastructure, poverty, violence, etc.), meetings (scheduled and unscheduled), attempting too much at one time, inability to say "no," buying into personal problems of staff, poorly organized staff members whose tasks were tied to mine, listening to the rumor mill, poor conferencing/interviewing techniques, use of inappropriate leadership style, open-door policy.

There are eight major categories of activities that you will experience and that must be considered as you reflect about time management and control of your school: (1) observing, supervising, and evaluating teachers; (2) meeting with parents and community groups; (3) planning and organizing the curriculum and total school program; (4) handling paperwork, reports, and daily mail; (5) working with support staff such as secretaries, custodians, and aides; (6) working through unexpected demands and crises; (7) responding to and working with district office personnel; and (8) hall duty and school grounds duty.

Operational procedures, rules, and policies—control mechanisms—are established to maintain school safety and security and to increase student achievement. Effective administrators define job roles, assign tasks, delegate appropriately, and require accountability. These behaviors are essential for meeting ISLLC Standard 3: The Management of Learning, whose areas of focus include organization, operations, resources, and safe schools. Artifacts that you may consider for the administrative portfolio appear in the Reflective Practice Exercises section at the end of this chapter.

THE VIRTUES OF THE ROUTINE ■

Routines and traditions are important tools for maintaining control in urban schools that serve as oasis for poor children whose lives are too frequently unpredictable and chaotic. Students want order—limits and support for following school rules and teachers' and other adults' directions. That is why it's imperative to include students as partners when establishing order in a disruptive school or in any school.

Although taking charge of and managing an urban school is a tall order, urban principals can and should make use of the various resources within the school community. Effective management is not a one-person undertaking. Moreover, the skills required demand that competencies be revisited and shared to ensure continuous improvement.

Warren Bennis (1994) reminds us that there are four competencies of leaders:

- Management of meaning
- Management of attention
- Management of trust
- Management of self

Management of Meaning

To be competent as an educational leader, one first must be able to manage the meaning of schooling. A leader has a clear understanding of the purpose of schools and can manage the symbols of the organization to fulfill that purpose.

Management of Attention

Management of attention is the educational leader's ability to get teachers to focus and expand their energies to fulfill the purpose of school—that is, to use their abilities to teach children.

Management of Trust

Management of trust means that leaders behave in such a way that others believe in them and the style of leadership does not become an issue.

Management of Self

Management of self is simply "I know who I am; I know my strengths and weaknesses. I play to my strengths and shore up my weaknesses."

As an urban school principal, you must make these four competencies a mantra that guides your actions. Keeping these competencies on your radar screen will prevent you from being distracted by false issues that cause you to react and behave in ways that do not contribute to leading an institution that is student centered, adult empowering, focused on continuous improvement, process managed, data driven, and outcomes based (see Figure 1.1).

■ CHOICE NOT CHANCE

Principals must choose to lead schools decisively with high expectations, high support, high content, and compassion. Management of schools cannot be left to chance.

Why not? Because schools have increased in size, legal and regulatory requirements have been added and have become more complex, and children need additional services to succeed academically. Moreover, the context of the principal's job has changed dramatically in the last 20 years. Doing this job successfully in today's schools means not only being able to unlock the instructional components well, but also recognizing the balance that is needed among a wide spectrum of responsibilities (Educational Research Service [ERS], 2000).

This balance of educational leadership, according to Strong (1993), is one that "draws a rational relationship between *managerial efficiency* and *instructionally effective schools*" (p. 5). A principal who focuses primarily on management issues may have insufficient time to provide instructional leadership, while a principal who neglects tasks that might be characterized as managerial does not provide the staff with a well-organized environment in which to work. Therefore, a characteristic

Figure 1.1   Characteristics of Successful Learning Institutions

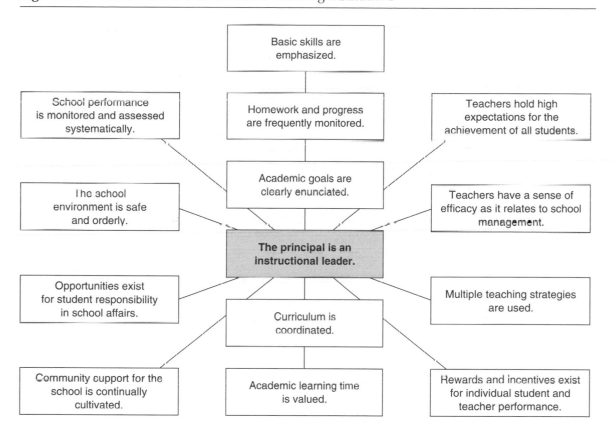

of the effective principal in today's urban schools must be the capacity to make decisions about, and focus on doing, what makes a difference—often on a daily basis (ERS, 2000).

LEADERSHIP STANDARDS AND EXPECTATIONS

Educators and policy makers have launched many helpful initiatives to redefine the roles of school leaders. The Council of Chief State School Officers, representatives from various professional associations, and representatives from 24 state education agencies cooperatively developed *Standards for School Leaders* (1996). The six standards present a common core of knowledge, dispositions, and performances that link leadership to productive schools and enhanced educational outcomes. Standard 3 focuses on the principal's management of the school: "A school administrator is an educational leader who promotes the success of all students by ensuring *management of the organization, operations, and resources for a safe, efficient, and effective learning environment* [italics added]" (p. 14).

Good leaders characteristically

manage reform activities   build consensus

delegate authority   secure participant buy-in

assume responsibility   gain bureaucratic support

These attributes underscore the overlap and importance of both instructional and management leadership behaviors of school principals.

Prior to the focus on explicit student socio-economic status and academic achievement data in conjunction with NCLB regulations, the U.S. Department of Education Blue Ribbon Schools' Program focused on 14 correlates of school effectiveness. Note that the expectation was that both instructional improvement and management support tasks were addressed by school leaders.

1. A principal who is an instructional leader
2. A safe and orderly school climate
3. An emphasis on basic skills
4. A system for monitoring and assessing school performance
5. Teachers with high expectations for the achievement of all students
6. The pronouncement of clear academic goals
7. A sense of teacher efficacy over the conduct of the school
8. Rewards and incentives for individual teachers and students
9. Community support for the school
10. Concentration on academic learning time
11. Emphasis on frequent and monitored homework
12. A coordinated curriculum
13. The use of a variety of teaching strategies
14. Opportunities for student responsibilities in school affairs

■ EXCELLENCE THEORY

Excellence theory focuses on management practices, pointing to those that may be linked to exemplary school outcomes in situations where an organization may have several layers, different types of administrators, and crosscutting organizational units. Peters and Waterman's *In Search of Excellence* (2004, 1982) contains an array of management practices that the authors claim have produced sustained excellent performance by a wide variety of businesses. The management practices include the following:

1. Having a bias for action
2. Being close to the customer
3. Preserving autonomy and entrepreneurship
4. Sustaining productivity through people
5. Being hands-on, value driven
6. Sticking to the knitting
7. Creating simple form, lean staff
8. Having simultaneous loose-tight properties

SOURCE: 8 Management Practices from *In Search of Excellence: Lessons From America's Best Run Companies* by Thomas J. Peters and Robert H. Waterman, Jr. Copyright © 1982, 2004 by Thomas J. Peters and Robert H. Waterman, Jr. Reprinted with permission of HarperCollins Publishers.

A firm had to be in the top half of its industry in at least four of six outcomes (three each for growth and income) over a 20-year period.

Think about what you do daily as an urban school principal with students, parents, teachers, and partners. Problems await you in the morning no matter what time you arrive. Either a student or teacher has arrived early, or the custodian is waiting because of some incident that occurred the night before with an employee, or a local police officer needs to speak with you. If you remain *customer focused*, you will count to 10 before saying, "There goes my 'to do list' for today!"

Practicing Leadership

To test the appropriateness of Peters and Waterman's management practices to what you do daily, try the following strategy when your day begins as described above.

1. Don't mistake the problem for a joint problem.

2. Ask, "Who is working for whom?"

3. After the person shares the problem with you, ask the person, "What do you think?" This leaves the next move up to the student or the subordinate because you have not accepted responsibility for the problem. If the person has a solution to the problem, listen to it. If it is a good one, tell the person to come back to you after the plan has been implemented. If the person does not have a solution, spend a few minutes going over the alternatives together, and then ask for his or her recommendation.

By following this strategy, you have employed management practices 1, 2, 3, and 4. Using the same situation, how does the "sticking to the knitting" criterion apply? Ask these questions: "Is there an instructional opportunity here?" and "Does this problem have a direct link to instruction?" If so, then it is appropriate for you to "stick to the knitting" in a number of different ways:

1. You may delegate the task to a teacher or an administrator.

2. You may add the item to the agenda for your next instructional council.

3. You may elect to place the item on your "to do list" and proceed as appropriate.

Excellence themes as translated to urban schools could also be interpreted as shown in Table 1.1.

EXCELLENCE IN SCHOOL LEADERSHIP ■

In *A Passion for Excellence*, Peters and Austin (1985) enlarge the focus, including a chapter directed at excellence in school leadership. Peters uses examples from the documented behavior of principals at Deerfield

Table 1.1   Excellence Themes in Urban School Management

Excellence Themes	*School Leadership/Management*
Having a bias for action	• Circulate in halls, classrooms • Use small groups for decisions, e.g., teams/grade levels/committees • Organize administrative teams • Observe teachers *teaching* daily
Being close to the customer	• Require end of quarter tests and provide feedback to students monthly • Conduct goal setting and midyear and end of the year conferences with all staff members • Meet with the student council monthly • Meet with parent groups monthly • Provide recognition and rewards for staff and students
Preserving autonomy and entrepreneurship	• Protect professional time • Support teachers' different teaching styles • Foster staff interaction across grade level and subjects (teaching across the curriculum)
Sustaining productivity through people	• Implement staff initiatives • Provide staff development • Conduct informal and formal observations and provide written and oral feedback
Being hands-on, value driven	• Gain consensus on goals/annual plan • Meet with faculty and staff monthly
Sticking to the knitting	• Concentrate on core curriculum
Maintaining quality control	• Hire only certified staff and/or provide financial support to get staff certified • Develop standardized categories for arriving at meaning of grades
Creating simple form, lean staff	• Hire few full-time administrators and nonteaching staff • Keep flat, nonmatrix organization
Having simultaneous loose-tight properties	• Mix central monitoring and school site decisions • Combine autonomy and shared goals • Maintain firm, fair discipline

Academy and the three "tough" urban schools in Sara Lawrence Lightfoot's study on high schools. The eight themes are reduced to three:

1. Superior customer service
2. Internal entrepreneurship
3. The facilitation of the first two with a "bone-deep" belief in the worth, dignity, and creative potential of every person in the organization

Using Peters's framework, Yin and White (1986) further document the applicability of *excellence theory* to the management of comprehensive urban secondary schools. In addition to the eight leadership practices already cited, they add this list of management practices:

Intensive and Personal Communication by the Principal

The ways to accomplish intensive and personal communication are as diverse as our 50 states. For some principals this means that the principal has an open-door policy and responds quickly to calls and requests from teachers and other staff members. For other principals this means that delegation becomes routine, so time becomes available for wandering.

This management practice may also require that you modify how you communicate with staff. You may decide to communicate with staff through other means than traditional faculty meetings. These might include department, grade level, or team meetings; brown bag lunches; informal conversations in the hallway; one-to-one conferences; memos, e-mail, and round-robin memos to a limited number of people; or copies of minutes, letters, reports, and executive summaries.

The Principal Acting as an Advocate for the School

Acting as an advocate for the school includes the following actions:

- Speaking at ministerial council meetings
- Participating in community forums
- Appearing as a guest on talk radio or community affairs programs
- Penning guest columns and writing letters to the editor about why partnerships and support by the public are essential for schools to fulfill their mission

Facilitating the following events helps to support your school:

- Mentoring programs (You should become the voice for mentoring programs. Mentoring programs cannot be successful if citizens from all walks of life do not step forward to fill mentoring slots.)
- Summer business internships for teachers (Such opportunities refine teachers' knowledge and skills and allow them to update their practices in keeping with new employment requirements for high school graduates.)
- Campaigns that provide financial support to student enrichment programs (Field trips to museums prepare students for becoming tomorrow's patrons of the arts, thereby ensuring the perpetuation of Western culture.)

Finally, being an advocate means developing an active school-community council that may result in the acquisition of resources for your school, including physical improvements to it.

Procedures for Streamlining the Routine Administration of the School

When you empower others to solve problems and make decisions—either individually or through teams, grade levels, or committees—you reduce layers of permission steps prior to action.

Steps to Protect Teaching Time and Professional Autonomy

Protecting teaching time and professional autonomy is easier to do than you think. Consider this list of strategies:

- Implement a 20-minute rule: students are not permitted to leave a classroom during the first 20 minutes of the period.
- Make schoolwide announcements on the public address system only twice a day, once in the morning and once in the afternoon.
- Reward teachers who are creative and whose students also score well on school district proficiency tests.
- Increase the length of the school day.
- Plan fewer assembly programs that all students are required to attend.
- Organize schools-within-a-school where teachers and students remain in one wing or area of the building. This cuts down on movement and increases teaching time.
- Relieve teachers of administrative duties.
- Schedule school rallies for after school.
- Encourage teachers to apply for external grants to develop new curricular materials.

Unlocking the Routine

Consider devising a list of five or six major practices in your school: afterschool detention, field trip permission, monthly assembly programs, cocurricular clubs, for example. Review the guidelines for implementation. Take the guidelines to a team, grade level, or committee meeting. Ask the group to revise the guidelines while maintaining accountability and quality service.

Ways to Promote Innovation and Variation in School Curriculum and Operations

By encouraging teachers, lead teachers, and guidance counselors to plan and teach units (interdisciplinary teaching), by using themes that appeal to students, and by encouraging staff to apply for grants to support such initiatives, you promote innovation and variation. You could also devise a school-based grant recognition program using school and/or PTA funds. Each semester teams of teachers could be recognized for their risk taking and creativity while implementing innovative strategies to increase student achievement. (Incentives might include certificates or money to be used either personally or for project implementation.)

Techniques for Hiring and Assigning Staff to Meet Existing School Goals

- Use incentives when hiring and assigning staff. For instance, reward teachers who agree to stay with your school and teach the agreed-upon subjects for at least five years. An incentive to do this could be payment of tuition for certification in the subjects they agree to teach.
- Implement looping. This can mean partnering seventh-grade mathematics teachers who lack skills in teaching algebra with a local teachers' college for further training. Teachers can take an algebra course in preparation for the next year's assignment.
- Develop your talent pool. Motivate long-term substitute teachers to become certified to teach. Be flexible with these staff members when it comes to the length of their workday. For instance, on some days allow them to leave work earlier than on other days. Consider paying teachers when they are absent and engaged in professional development (attending a workshop, completing work in the college library, etc.).
- Be flexible.

Frequent Monitoring of Staff and Provision of Inservice Opportunities

The school staff development committee can plan, develop, monitor, and evaluate all inservice staff development sessions. Connect these activities to the annual school objectives. Serving on such a committee requires a lot of time; draft teachers to serve if necessary.

When observing every teacher during the first and fourth quarters each year, follow the master school schedule for students at each grade level. Students are often excited by the prospect of having the principal with them for the seven-period day. If students take physical education, change clothes and participate in the physical education activities. Follow up by providing teachers with a joint memorandum about your observations. The memorandum should focus on the quality of teaching, student management and discipline, and record keeping, including the following items:

- Student work folders and portfolios
- The classroom's physical appearance (desk arrangements, cleanliness, shades on windows drawn or up, etc.)
- The existence of instructional-focused bulletin boards
- Student posted, graded work

If, for example, you observe the use of ineffective teaching practices, give the teacher evidence of this practice in an individual memorandum as well.

A second monitoring strategy is to visit classrooms for five to ten minutes and leave a "kudos card" encouraging the teacher to keep up the good work. Teachers often enjoy a visit from the principal and consider

---

Unlocking Successful Monitoring Strategies

Carry kudos cards (cards with positive sayings on them), school buttons, and school tee shirts with you so when students respond correctly to some math problem, historical fact, or school-related question you ask, you can immediately give them a reward from your stash.

Unlocking Enhanced Visibility

- Man the cafeteria period (most principals don't).
- Visit all floors and areas of your building twice a day.
- Observe and provide oral and written feedback to teachers.
- Attend departmental, team, and grade-level meetings (provide written feedback about the meetings).
- Sponsor quarterly "bag lunch" time with teams of teachers.
- Participate on an all-school hospitality committee.
- Attend funerals and visit hospitalized teachers.

Unlocking the Ability to Learn From Mistakes

Permit those persons to whom you have delegated authority or decision making to make their own mistakes. Sometimes the best decisions are made by the people closest to the problem. At intervals, staff should pause and assess what is working and what is not. The assessment is called "Lessons Learned So Far."

---

the visit a needed break, especially if the principal can engage the students for a few minutes in some type of academic or school spirit activity.

Sustaining Frequent and Informal Staff Interactions and Communication

Don't think that you have to have an open-door policy as principal. Conferences should be scheduled. However, teachers and staff should know that if a situation arises and they feel they really need to see you, they are free to come right in. Teachers and staff are not likely to abuse this policy if you are visible in the school.

Mixed Control Monitoring and Decentralized Decision Making

Delegate to assistant principals and department heads, and encourage them to involve all teachers on their floor or in their departments in decision making and implementation. Encourage the assistant principal or the department head to "find out what makes that person tick" if a particular teacher remains uninvolved. They should use what they learn about the person to engage and involve that person.

A comprehensive theory of school leadership must embrace both instructional management and organizational management, each reflecting excellence.

In a series of five meetings in the winter of 1996–1997, five forums on urban education sponsored by the U. S. Department of Education, the Council of the Great City Schools, and the Institute for Educational Leadership resulted in strategies for improving urban education. These strategies affirm the importance of principals' and other district leaders' management behaviors (Council of the Great City Schools, 1999):

- Set fewer, clearer goals focused on challenging academic standards.
- Strengthen supports for teachers and leaders.

- Develop a school climate conducive to learning.
- Establish stronger collective accountability for school performance.
- Increase investments in urban education.
- Build on what works.

PROBLEMS OF PRACTICE ◼

Nine "problems of practice" are discussed in the book *City Schools: Leading the Way* (1993) by Forsyth and Tallerico. The problems were identified by a specially selected group of successful city principals, metropolitan youth-serving professionals, and urban university faculty.

- Understanding the urban context and conditions of practice
- Motivating urban children to learn
- Building open climates in urban schools
- Collecting and using information for decision making
- Managing instructional diversity
- Acquiring and using urban resources
- Governing urban schools
- Effecting change in urban schools
- Establishing mission, vision, and goals

In the chapter focusing on student engagement, Forsyth and Tallerico (1993) discuss two overlapping frameworks that focus on the school while they help analyze the motivation problems. One approach is to examine the organizational structures of the school for possible alienating effects on urban children. For example, consider a school policy that penalizes students for lateness. If school staff are aware that a student is late because he has to see that his sibling reaches elementary school before he reports to school, perhaps the solution is not to provide the student with an alarm clock so that he gets to school on time, but rather to devise an individual school schedule for the student so that his school day begins later. This strategy could be used with a large number of students. The school's goal is to increase student attendance, and students need to be present to master the content taught. The schedule revision accomplishes both goals.

The other approach is for the principal to concentrate his or her attention on creating a task-focused learning environment. This example points to other educational research that focuses on principals' strategic options. It is not unusual for urban principals to be reluctant to direct or require that everyone complete some task in a specific way. This is as it should be; however, it is not unreasonable. In fact, it is your job to require that people adhere to time allotments for instruction because the research says learning is increased by 70% when you do. Time on task is not optional in urban schools in which student achievement is exceptionally low. Teachers should be encouraged to identify ways in which they can increase instructional time on task and reduce discipline management strategies.

Using Transformational and Facilitative Approaches

Urban principals may choose among several strategic options that will lead them down very different paths. Is there a "best" strategy? Much of the current literature, according to Smith and Piele (2006), seems to favor transformational and facilitative approaches, but wise administrators will try to distinguish enthusiastic advocacy from objective evidence. Beck and Murphy (1993) point out that metaphors for school leadership come and go. Just since 1960, principals have been asked to be efficient bureaucrats, scientific managers, humanistic educators, instructional leaders, and now transformational/facilitative leaders. The authors further observe that prevailing images may say more about the preoccupations of society than the inherent needs of schools.

■ PROFESSIONAL DEVELOPMENT OPTIONS

As a new or newly reassigned urban school principal, you will continually employ a variety of strategies to assist you in becoming an effective leader. What are some professional development options? Consider these possibilities:

- Read books on leadership and organizational theories.
- Attend courses and principal academies.
- Participate in your school district.
- Use the state's or a national association's assessment center.
- Secure a mentor.
- Engage in peer coaching experiences.
- Self-administer leadership style inventories.

The first step for urban school leaders wanting to improve their leadership style is to become aware of what their style is. This seemingly simple task turns out to be complicated. The Resource section of this book provides a matrix of leadership style instruments that should prove helpful as you explore various styles for various purposes. Proceed with caution, however, when using personal assessment measures. They are not perfect. You should not be too quick to embrace the judgment of any instrument. The pros and cons of the instruments' reliability and validity are as varied as the instruments themselves.

■ CONTROL SURVEYS FOR SCHOOL ASSESSMENT USE

As the newly assigned urban school principal, you want to execute three levels of behaviors: initiate; stabilize; and sustain effective practices, initiatives, and programs in the school. Included with the Reflective Practice Exercises at the end of this chapter are several surveys to guide your practice. Using these surveys will help you to be proactive and decisive.

Establishing control and managing the school is not easy. But it is required if the principal's vision and the school district's expectations are to be achieved. As the person in charge, the principal uses sensitivity skills and exercises judgment judiciously while recognizing that decisiveness is critical during the early stage of making his or her presence known.

CONTROL REFLECTIVE PRACTICE EXERCISES

Control

Reflective Practice Exercise #1

Consider the following questions. Write your answers below each.

1. To whom should a student report the existence of a weapon on school property?

2. If a parent is uncertain about his or her child's eligibility to take an advanced placement course in chemistry, whom should he or she ask for assistance?

3. What are the school's rules about students wearing tee shirts with inappropriate messages?

4. If a teacher has a cardiac arrest in the hallway, what are those who observe the teacher's collapse to do?

Answers to these types of questions should be found in one or more of three documents in your school:

- The student handbook
- The faculty and staff handbook
- The parent handbook

However, if these documents do not exist or if they are not distributed and discussed with the audiences for whom they are designed, schools can be disruptive, disorderly, and dangerous places in which to learn and to work.

Control

Reflective Practice Exercise #2

INITIATING CONTROL

Goal: To exercise leadership and facilitate the orderly operation of the school.

Document	Exists	Everyone Has	Needs Revision	Is Reviewed Formally at Least Twice Yearly
Faculty/Staff Handbook				
Student Handbook				
Parent Handbook				
School Calendar (Monthly and/or Yearly)				
Volunteer/Business Partnership Handbook				
Code of Conduct Posted				
Daily/Weekly Bulletin				
Sign-Up Sheet for Use of Common Areas				
School Spirit/Climate				
Circulars/Memos/Policy				
Administrative Regulation (Binder easily accessible for staff's use)				
Parent Group Communications Notebook				

Answer the following questions based on your inventory:

1. How many documents on the list exist in your school?

2. How many documents need revision?

3. Who developed the documents? Is there a reference that identifies the contributors or developers?

4. Is there a review process for each document? How do you know this to be true?

5. How is the faculty/staff handbook distributed to staff? Is this document signed out each fall and returned to school administrators at the end of each school year? If yes, are revisions made yearly?

6. How are these documents distributed?

If there are no handbooks for substitute teachers, volunteers, and business partners, appoint a committee and have these developed. To initiate control of volunteers and business partners is imperative. Both sectors will have a tremendous impact on the reputation of your school. People talk about their school experiences—pleasant or unpleasant. Do not leave your school's reputation to chance with these two sectors.

Your time and that of your assistant principal can be inappropriately expended when the documents listed are not available. A more productive use of your time could ensure time for instructional supervision or for a variety of other tasks that would impact student achievement.

Control

Reflective Practice Exercise #3

Initiating control in a school extends beyond the existence of documents. The existence of a student activities program that reaches out to all segments of the student population can contribute significantly to the following:

- School climate
- Student academic achievement
- Student scholarships
- Students' participation in competitions and contests
- A host of other correlates to school effectiveness, such as parent involvement

The existence of administrative monitoring systems for attendance, suspension, and expulsion enables school administrators to use accurate numerical data on a moment's notice.

The reception parents and visitors receive from school staff is more important than a professionally prepared pamphlet extolling the exceptional academic and athletic programs in your school. Thus, training and monitoring secretarial and other support staff assigned to administrative offices throughout the school are paramount, as is celebrating excellent performance.

A dirty school and school grounds with debris are uninviting for students, teachers, staff, parents, and other visitors. Moreover, students do not respect schools in which the adults do not make them feel welcome and respected. Physical appearance and emotional support count! Bare classrooms, no classroom library, no plants, no colorful posters, no student work posted, outdated tattered books or no books, broken or missing instructional equipment, empty bulletin boards or bulletin boards that aren't changed regularly all say to students, "You do not matter. You are not important."

When such negative conditions exist, principals are compelled to exhibit leadership behavior attributed to charismatic leaders: a sense of purpose and a sense of optimism that is specific and directive.

Answer the questions below about your school. An action plan or plans should be developed to turn every statement that received a "no" into a "yes."

INITIATING CONTROL

Activities	Yes	No
These student groups exist, are affiliated with state and national groups, or are representative of the student body. __ student council __ honor society __ Pan-Hellenic council __ newspaper staff	☐	☐
Students compete in at least three (local, state, regional) contests.	☐	☐
Monitoring systems to capture daily attendance (staff and students), suspensions, and expulsions are in place.	☐	☐
All administrative offices are warm and friendly reception areas for parents, teachers, students, and visitors.	☐	☐
Clerical staff have been trained how to answer the telephone and greet visitors.	☐	☐
Quarterly open house is held (providing opportunities for parent/ community visits).	☐	☐
The school is safe, clean, and inviting (colorful posted student work, slogans, plants throughout the school, etc.).	☐	☐
School grounds are free of paper and other debris.	☐	☐
A plan exists to educate all staff in critical areas such as AIDS, reporting child abuse, sexual harassment, teen pregnancy, drug abuse, teenage suicide, etc.	☐	☐

Control

Reflective Practice Exercise #4

STABILIZING CONTROL

Let's turn our attention to the Stabilizing Control Survey below. If you are not a new principal but are newly assigned to a school that is in need of a "different" kind of leadership, it is important that you assess sound management practices that say to employees, "We are about academic achievement, developmental responsiveness, and equity practices that include contributions from all sectors and attention to rewarding excellence." Although not exhaustive, the survey contains key practices for stabilizing control in a school. If you are a newly assigned principal, do not get overexcited about the variety of practices. You cannot implement every effective practice that you would like to during the first three years of your assignment in a school. Review the list with the idea of sharing it with selected faculty members or a study group. The transformation of a school is not a one-year, one-person undertaking. However, your leadership is critical.

	Yes	No
Documents are reviewed formally at least twice yearly. (Purpose: To check for understanding and to reinforce policy. Documents include all handbooks. Times: September, January)	☐	☐
For "new" students and staff, documents are given to and reviewed with them within two weeks of enrollment/employment.	☐	☐
A buddy system exists for all "new" students and staff.	☐	☐
Academic assemblies (whole school/grade level/teams) are held at least twice a year.	☐	☐
Assembly programs that require critical listening skills and acceptable audience politeness are held periodically.	☐	☐
There is a recognition program for exemplary performance (developed with input from recipients) for	☐	☐

__ faculty and staff   __ students   __ parents

__ volunteers and partners

	Yes	No
Parent/teacher/student report card conferences are held at least twice yearly.	☐	☐
Teachers are encouraged to attend professional development workshops and conferences.	☐	☐
There is a school song. Students and staff know it and it is sung on a regular basis, e.g., opening exercise, assembly programs, athletic activities	☐	☐
Teachers are required to enrich the curriculum by taking students on field trips.	☐	☐
Teachers are required to have posted daily objectives for lessons and "to do" or drill activities for students to complete upon arrival.	☐	☐
There is a reward system for recognizing perfect and improved attendance (staff and students).	☐	☐

Control

Reflective Practice Exercise #5

SUSTAINING EDUCATIONAL IMPROVEMENT

To sustain educational improvement, practices are fewer but equally important. Implementing these practices will move you closer to reaching the school's vision of excellence. Complete the survey and discuss the results with one or all of the following groups: school site council, building leadership team, administrative leadership team, department heads/grade level chairpersons, PTA/PTSO. Develop a plan to give life to prioritized activities. Good luck!

	Yes	No
Eighty percent of faculty meeting agenda items deal with instructional issues.	☐	☐
One-third of the faculty participate in professional development activities that result in pilot projects in the school, e.g., clusters, departments, teaching teams.	☐	☐
Academic assemblies are held quarterly.	☐	☐
Every discipline has students who participate in local, state, and national competitions.	☐	☐
Coach classes are held by every teacher.	☐	☐
Classified staff participate in professional development activities.	☐	☐

2

Caring

*Addressing the Affective Domain
of Leadership Success*

The telephone rings constantly at the Lemmel Middle School office. Every time it's answered with the greeting "Lemmel, a school for winners. May I help you?" or "It's a great day at Lemmel Middle School. May I help you?" The staff focuses on not making the caller wait on hold for more than two minutes. When parents or other visitors arrive at the office counter, they are entitled to and receive a warm "Glad you are here" greeting by staff.

A large bulletin board in the lobby is devoted to topics of interest to parents and families. When visitors are asked to wait, they can sit apart from the students who may also be waiting. The students are engaged in constructive activities such as reading or doing homework as they wait.

Greeting parents promptly and with respect and seeing the school from a parent's perspective conveys an attitude that parents are welcome participants in their child's education. It also sends a message that the school cares about what parents think. A school that welcomes parents evidences effective management.

AFFECTIVE ASPECTS OF THE STANDARDS-BASED SCHOOL ENVIRONMENT

For the past decade, educators, elected officials, business and community leaders, and members of the general public have conducted an intense debate on how to raise and enforce higher standards and improve education generally. But much of the discussion omits two critical elements: the motivation and behavior of the students, and affective aspects of a standards-based school environment. Two exceptions to this generalization stand out: *Getting By: What American Teenagers Really Think About Their Schools* (an opinion poll conducted and published by Public Agenda, 1997) and *Breaking Ranks: Changing an American Institution* (commissioned and published by the National Association of Secondary School Principals, 1996).

What Students Think

When administrators are attempting to personalize schools, students' opinions are key to both the discussion and the subsequent recommendations for changes in policies, practices, and procedures.

In *Getting By*, students answered 11 questions that focused on different kinds of teachers and how much students learned based on the teachers' behaviors. The results of this survey make it clear that effort counts with the students. What is also clear is that teachers' initiative and compassion are equally important.

Sixty-nine percent of the teens said they would learn "a lot more" from a teacher who treats them with respect or takes the time to provide individual help. About two-thirds said they respond well to a teacher who challenges them to do better and learn more (66%), explains lessons very carefully (66%), or cares about them (64%). What implications for the principal's behaviors result from these student beliefs?

IMPORTANCE OF AFFECTIVE FOCUS IN SCHOOL REFORM

Two national reports stand out for their focus on establishing learning communities that acknowledge the growth and change, physically, emotionally, and socially, that adolescents experience in the middle and high school years. Thus, major recommendations in each address the affective domain that has significant implications for school leaders.

In *Turning Points* (1989), the Carnegie Council on Adolescent Development Task Force on Education of Young Adolescents recommends that middle grade schools create small communities for learning in which stable, close, mutually respectful relationships with adults and peers are considered fundamental for intellectual development and personal growth. The key elements of these communities are schools within schools, or houses: students and teachers grouped together as teams with small group advisors who ensure that every student is known well by at least one adult.

In *Breaking Ranks: Changing an American Institution* (1996), the National Association of Secondary School Principals' Commission on the

Restructuring of the American High School affirms that better education depends on personalizing the high school experience for students. Therefore, adults must demonstrate that they care about students in a variety of ways. Specifically, the commission recommends that high schools break into units of no more than 600 students so that teachers and students can get to know each other better. Then teachers should use a variety of instructional strategies that accommodate individual learning styles and engage students. To achieve this goal, every student should have a personal adult advocate and a personal plan for progress.

To nudge principals to implement the recommendations of both groups, the secondary principals' association organized two Alliances of Schools and provided products (an Alliance newsletter and monographs) and services (a network directory on the Internet, regional conferences, special events at the NASSP Convention) to assist member schools with implementation.

As part of the National Association of Secondary School Principals' committee structure, the Urban Schools Committee was asked to brainstorm a list of typical behaviors that demonstrate that "principals·care about students and staff in their schools." Box 2.1 summarizes the subgroup's work. Not surprisingly, the list mirrors some, but not all, behaviors advocated in *Turning Points* and *Breaking Ranks*.

Unlocking the Affective Domain Through Administrative Action

- Establish small learning groups.
- Foster mutually respectful relationships with adults and peers.
- Assign small group advisors.
- Ensure that every student is known well by at least one adult.
- Personalize school experiences for students.
- Accommodate individual learning styles.

■ INVITING SCHOOL SUCCESS

In his book *I Won't Learn From You,* Herbert R. Kohl concludes that students' unwillingness or refusal to be molded by a society they perceive to be hostile can be "positive and healthy in many situations" (Kohl, 1991, p. 2). Kohl calls this conscious decision by some students "not learning." Not learning cannot be considered a passive act. On the contrary, it "is an intellectual and social challenge" that is inherent in many students' self-respect and identity (p. 32).

What are some behaviors that urban school principals need to exhibit to ensure that few students choose not to learn in their schools?

Box 2.1   Principals' Caring Behaviors

- Knows the names of students, teachers, and other staff members
- Pronounces people's names correctly
- Speaks to everybody on a regular basis
- Acknowledges students' and adults' accomplishments

- Is visible
- Is available (Being visible does not guarantee availability.)
- Asks/shows concern about students' and adults' personal problems
- Implements student recognition programs
- Demonstrates patience
- Is a good listener
- Encourages others to achieve at high levels
- Is involved
- Reinforces others for tasks completed well
- Uses nonverbal communication that is positively reinforcing
- Ensures that people get needed resources by seeing that necessary social services are located in the school or easily accessed
- Reaches out
- Implements recognition and awards programs
- Is flexible
- Lives in the community where the students live
- Responds quickly to people's requests
- Organizes the school so that students and adults get to know each other

Essential to the above caring behaviors is the urban school principal's knowledge and use of invitational leadership strategies that may advance a school climate that nurtures both students and adults—parents, certified staff, and noncertified staff. Invitational leadership is defined as "an attempt to focus an educator's desires, understandings and actions in order to create a total school environment that appreciates individuals' uniqueness and calls forth their potential" (Novak, 2005, p. 46).

According to Novak (2005), an invitation is defined as the "summary of the content of messages communicated verbally, non-verbally, formally and informally *through* people, places, policies, programmes and processes" (p. 46). These inviting messages tell people they are valuable, able, and responsible and can behave accordingly. Urban schools come alive or are deadened by the messages communicated through the five focus areas—people, places, policies, programmes, and processes—identified by Novak. The reader is encouraged to read Novak's works since only the focus on people is addressed herein.

Urban school principals' awareness of the invitations students receive from adults—other administrators, teachers, social workers, psychologists, the nurse, the school secretaries, the bus driver, the custodian, cafeteria workers—during the course of a school day is critical to understanding the social-emotional climate of the school. According to William Purkey (1996), four levels of invitations are usually apparent in schools (see Figure 2.1):

Level 1: intentionally disinviting

Level 2: unintentionally disinviting

Level 3: unintentionally inviting

Level 4: intentionally inviting

Figure 2.1   Purkey's Levels of Inviting

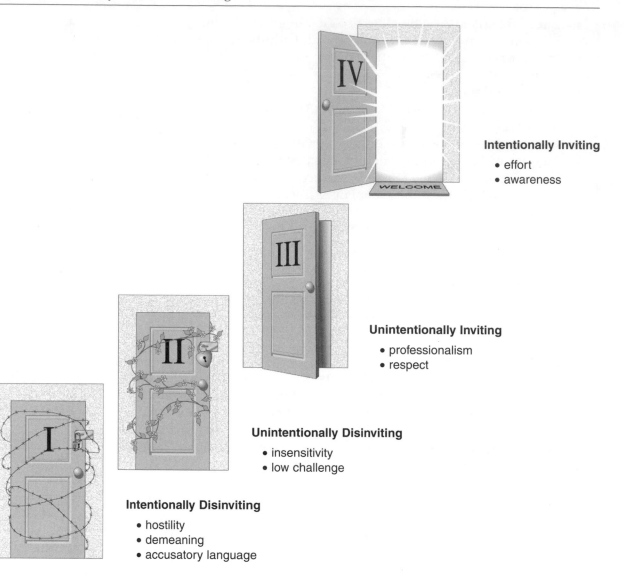

Intentionally Inviting
- effort
- awareness

Unintentionally Inviting
- professionalism
- respect

Unintentionally Disinviting
- insensitivity
- low challenge

Intentionally Disinviting
- hostility
- demeaning
- accusatory language

SOURCE: Adapted from Purkey & Novak, *Inviting School Success.* © 1978 Wadsworth, an imprint of the Wadsworth Group, division of Thomson Learning.

While all educators function at all levels from time to time, most teachers appear to function at one level more than others. It will be helpful to consider these four levels briefly.

Level 1: Intentionally Disinviting

Some teachers and school personnel spend considerable time informing students that they are incapable, worthless, and irresponsible. Whether because of racial prejudice, unrequited love, personal inadequacy, sadistic impulse, or negative self-image, certain people in the helping professions function at the intentionally disinviting level. It is the principal's responsibility to recommend professional help for these people. If this fails, it is the principal's duty to remove them from daily contact with students.

Level 2: Unintentionally Disinviting

Unintentionally disinviting teachers are usually well meaning and high-minded, but their teaching methods belie their good intentions. Their teaching is usually characterized by boredom, "busy work," and insensitivity to feelings. Teachers' behaviors perceived by students as chauvinistic, condescending, or patronizing are likely to be interpreted as disinvitation regardless of the teacher's intention.

Level 3: Unintentionally Inviting

Just as it is possible to be friendly without being a friend, so it is possible to be inviting without sending an invitation. Probably many so-called natural-born teachers, those who have never taken a professional education course but who are highly effective in the classroom, are successful because they are unintentionally inviting. They typically behave in ways that result in student feelings of being invited, although they remain unaware of the dynamics involved.

Level 4: Intentionally Inviting

Teachers should try to be intentionally inviting. The more explicit an invitation, the more it lends itself to evaluation, direction, and modification. To illustrate, one student writes,

> Miss Penn always used our real names when speaking to us. Other teachers might call you "honey" or "sweetheart," but Miss Penn always called us by our real names. She told us at the beginning of the year that she had difficulty in remembering names, so if she called us by the wrong name, not to get upset. She said that when she used a real name, even if it was the wrong one, it showed us that she was trying to learn each student's name. We appreciated that. (Purkey, 1996, pp. 16–20)

PERSONALIZING SCHOOLS TO MEET STUDENTS' NEEDS

Children and youth need invitations the way flowers need sunshine. When they are treated with indifference, they are likely to become indifferent to themselves and to school. They begin to say to themselves, "Give up; no one cares about how well I did this." What it means is that students who have learned to feel bad about themselves as learners are vulnerable to additional failure, just as a physically weak person is susceptible to illness.

The size of your student population should not deter the assistant principal(s) and you from knowing a significant number of students by name. Administrators' presence at certain predictable times of the school day gives students a sense of security and an

Unlocking a Culture of Caring

The caring for students loudly proclaims the following

- You matter!
- Your thoughts and ideas matter!
- You are expected to excel academically, socially, emotionally, and physically!
- The school's array of options that involve you, your parents, the teachers, and community members all indicate how much we care and how much you matter!

Unlocking MBWA (Managing by Walking Around)

Look at your calendar for the last 60 days. Break it down into hall duty, cafeteria duty, classroom observations, pre- and post-observation conferences, student programs, organized sports activities, and meetings. (Meetings should be subdivided into administrative, grade level, cluster, department head, classified staff, parents, school site team, etc.) Make notes on the location of each meeting. Ask yourself whether a meeting that took place in your office could have taken place as readily on the other person's turf.

Now look ahead for the next 30 days. First look at booked, must-do events. Can some be held at "their place" rather than at "your place"? Look at your currently unprogrammed time; can you put "Don't book" in 25% of it and save the time for spontaneous wandering?

---

opportunity for administrators to circulate and learn students' names.

Regular interaction with and on behalf of students, with students' knowledge, promotes organizational values. Through caring activities specifically aimed at students, school administrators are determining the organizational culture. Culture can be described as basic assumptions a group uses to cope with its problems. The culture, then, is a prism through which the organization's members perceive challenges. In short, an organization's culture is how things are done around here.

Values

The school's values have a profound impact on its operations. For example, values will determine the following practices:

- Whether academics or athletics are given high priority
- Whether girls and minorities can obtain formal leadership positions
- The importance of advanced placement courses
- The importance of English as a second language
- The things to which employees are willing to devote extra time and effort

■ MANAGING BY WALKING AROUND

How can we create additional conditions that demonstrate our caring in concrete ways? Managing by Walking Around (MBWA) is one additional way to demonstrate caring for one's student body and the faculty and staff.

MBWA is not a passive, uninvolved strategy. In addition to the physical exertion, as the effective leader wanders, he or she coaches, develops, and engenders small wins. A lot is going on—at least three major activities: listening, teaching, and facilitating (Peters & Austin, 1985). Regardless of the school size and the student population, every urban school principal should practice MBWA.

Frequency is critical to MBWA. If you are not a frequent wanderer, the onset of wandering will terrify you and those with whom you come in contact. Scheduled classroom observations or attendance at grade-level or department meetings seldom bear a direct relationship to reality. People stage events, and the most vital function of MBWA, listening, is not accomplished effectively. The best way to augment preplanned, prescheduled observations and meetings is by wandering often, regularly, every day of the 180-day school year. If you are a middle/junior high or senior high school principal, how about shadowing a sixth- or ninth-grade student one day, a seventh- or tenth-grade student the next day, an eighth- or eleventh-grade student the third day, and a senior the fourth day? You will learn volumes! Elementary principals might stay with a class all day (shadowing a specific student) if classes are self-contained and students do not move to different teachers for instruction in specific content areas. The same strategy would be used for observing special education students.

Yes, it will be awkward at first. You are "inconveniencing" yourself to climb four flights of stairs daily. Additionally, why should any staff member or students be interested or committed to giving you honest feedback if your last three interactions were to discipline them? Do not expect people to give you what you are looking for initially. You earn honest feedback, and the main way you earn it is by the frequency of your wandering. This frequency says to everyone, "The principal cares!"

> ### Unlocking the Heart of Leadership
>
> Think about how you interact with and validate the behaviors of teachers and other adults in the school. These interactions speak to how the school climate reflects the school's mission and provides an atmosphere that is conducive to learning. Just as schools can be disinviting to students, they can be disinviting to teachers and other adults as well. For example, an invitation to confer about instructional goals for one's classroom and professional goals for oneself may be personally motivational and inviting for a teacher. A staff person might welcome your endorsement that he or she should establish a partnership with the local social worker who works with foster children in the school. Consult Reflective Practice Exercises 4, 5, and 6 at the end of this chapter to begin thinking more deeply about this topic.

BEING UP FRONT AND PERSONAL WITH FACULTY AND STAFF CULTURE

Sergiovanni (1990a) proposed that the type of quality control being advocated here is more cultural than managerial. When one stabilizes caring and enriches it so that adults routinely see themselves and students as part of the solution and not as part of the problem, "the minds and ears of people are at work" (p. 10). It has to do with what teachers and other school employees believe, their commitment to quality, their sense of pride, the extent to which they identify with their work, the ownership they feel for what they are doing, and the intrinsic satisfaction they derive from the work itself. Quality control characterized by caring is "purposing, enablement, leadership density, collegiality, and intrinsic motivation as means to build identity and commitment" (p. 12).

In *Shaping School Culture: The Heart of Leadership* (1998), Deal and Peterson state that school leaders can shape culture over time in the following ways:

- Develop a student-centered mission and purpose that motivates the heads and hearts of staff, students, and community.

- Strengthen elements of the existing culture that are positive and supportive of core values.
- Build on established traditions and values, adding new constructive ones to the existing combination.
- Recruit, hire, and socialize staff who share the values of the culture and who will add new insights or skills to the culture.
- Use the history (or build the history if the school is new) of the culture to fortify the core values and beliefs.
- Sustain core norms, values, and beliefs in everything the school does.

■ ON BECOMING A SOULFUL SCHOOL

Quoting Secretan, (1996) in *Education and the Soul,* John P. Miller (2000) defines the soulful organization as a sanctuary, for example, an integrated system of souls—a state of mind where souls may flourish. In the sanctuary, people's feelings, as well as their thoughts, are acknowledged. Both teachers and students look forward to being at school as they feel that the environment they find there nourishes their souls. This environment is one of respect, caring, and even reverence. People in the soulful school feel validated as human beings and can speak authentically from their hearts. Love predominates rather than fear. When people speak, they feel that they are heard, often at a heart-centered level. Most of all, there is a deep sense of community.

Miller enumerates many strategies that develop a sanctuary, or a soulful school. As the school principal, you not only can practice the strategies that follow, but your modeling and stated expectations that staff do likewise will go a long way to give life to the expression "caring turns into miracles every day." Notice the overlap between several suggestions here and those enumerated by Deal and Peterson earlier. According to Miller (2000), some of the things that you and your staff can do include the following:

Recognize the importance of the nonverbal. When we focus on the nonverbal, we become aware of how we carry ourselves, how we engage others through eye contact, and the tone of our voice. We realize that the quality of our being and presence has as much impact on student development as anything that we say.

Pay attention to the aesthetic environment of the school and classroom. Make the physical environment more beautiful. For example, plants can become a part of the school decor in the halls and in the classrooms. Student and professional artwork can be placed on the walls.

Tell stories about the school. The stories eventually can create a mythology for the school. This mythology is a shared sense of meaning and values for the school.

Have celebrations and rituals. This suggestion is closely related to the last one. Rituals help give people a sense of connection to their communities.

Celebrations could be conducted to mark changes in the seasons. Rituals can be part of the daily life of the school. Each morning you might begin the day with a quotation, meditation, or short story that everyone would keep in mind during the course of the day.

Truth and Authenticity. When we live in an atmosphere in which people are not telling the truth, integrity and community break down. One behavior that helps build authenticity is promise keeping. When we keep our promises, others can learn to depend on our word. Sometimes in schools, gaps develop between what we espouse and what we do.

Nourishing Voice. A soulful, caring school is a place where people can speak without fear.

Use various curriculum approaches and teaching/learning strategies. The ways described in Miller's (2000) book include a curriculum for the inner life, use of the arts, earth education, service learning, use of meditation (a controversial strategy), and guided imagery. Use of authentic assessment helps to provide evidence of how the student is doing.

Urban school principals' *caring* behaviors are not to be limited to interactions with students and teachers. Parents, other school staff (cafeteria workers, custodians, secretaries, etc.) and school volunteers are important stakeholders who are the messengers who make a difference to the public relations of your schools. The conversations these people have in barber shops and salons, while shopping in department and grocery stores, and while meeting in their synagogues, mosques, and churches determine your school's reputation. More important than this, however, is the fact that these stakeholders are important participants in the educational process and deserve your respect, support, and recognition of the contributions that they make to your school being the positive, validating place where wonderful memories are made and relived a thousand times!

> **Unlocking the Ability to Be Up Front and Personal**
>
> How do you get up front and personal with your faculty and staff? Is knowing them as important to you as knowing the student population? Why or why not? Discuss Reflective Practice Exercise 6 with your administrative team. If you do not have an administrative team, discuss it with a fellow principal. Are the recommended activities doable in your school? Why or why not? For the doable activities, whom do you need to assist you to ensure that they are executed on a regular basis? Can any of the activities be delegated to an assistant principal? If yes, how will you monitor?

CARING REFLECTIVE PRACTICE EXERCISES

Caring

Reflective Practice Exercise #1

Review each of the strategies you read about in this chapter and think about the answers to the questions that follow. Revisit the list from time to time as you think about the climate in your school and the importance of your role as a Leader Who Cares.

- What tone of voice do you hear as you manage by walking around? Do the tones nurture the soul? If not, what are you going to do about this?

- Are live plants located throughout the school? Who brought the plants into the school? Who cares for the plants? Besides people, what other living things are in the school? Are there lessons to be learned about "caring" with many "alive" things in the school?

- Who tells stories about the school on a regular basis? What is the nature of these stories?

- Does every classroom from time to time celebrate some accomplishment or recognize some important event?

- Are students comfortable asking questions and/or challenging adult positions/pronouncements in a respectful manner? Do students approach you regularly with questions?

- Are a variety of assessment tools used to see how students are performing? Are there opportunities for community service within and outside the school?

- Are students active participants in designing and implementing the character education curriculum? Are they involved in developing the code of conduct for their acceptable behavior?

Caring

Reflective Practice Exercise #2

INITIATING CARING (STUDENTS)

Determine whether or not the statements that follow accurately reflect your school's level of caring. For those statements you find do not reflect what your school is currently doing, undertake an action plan in concert with your governing team to increase your school's caring quotient.

Goal: To promote and maintain a strong personal relationship with the student body.

	Yes	No
Students are addressed by name by teachers, administrators, and support staff.	☐	☐
Students are greeted/welcomed to school/class daily by school administrators (on duty at front entrance) and teachers (at door of classroom).	☐	☐
Students can identify at least five adults to whom they can go for assistance (e.g., principal, assistant principal, counselor, teacher, school police).	☐	☐
Coach classes are available to students who need them.	☐	☐
An emergency fund is available to purchase needed supplies and/or a system is in place to provide students with school supplies.	☐	☐
A range of course offerings are available.	☐	☐

- Standard
- Advanced Placement
- Remediation
- Vocational

The principal meets with the student council leadership group monthly.	☐	☐
Partnerships exist with social service agencies, juvenile justice departments, and advocacy groups to address student needs that the school is not equipped to address.	☐	☐

Caring

Reflective Practice Exercise #3

STABILIZING CARING (STUDENTS)

Determine whether or not the statements that follow accurately reflect your school's level of caring. For those statements you find do not reflect what your school is currently doing, undertake an action plan in concert with your governing team to increase your school's caring quotient.

Goal: To promote academic excellence and well-roundedness in students.

	Yes	No
Cheating is defined in the student handbook.	☐	☐
There is an honor roll for academic achievement, which is conspicuously displayed, is changed more than once yearly, and typically lists between 5% and 25% of the pupils.	☐	☐

These student activities exist in the school and at least 50% of the student body are active participants. Check all that apply.

__academic teams/clubs	__office assistant, messengers
__band	__monitors and/or hall guards
__choir	__community service
__cheerleading	__drama club
__fundraising out of	__debating team
school (e.g., walkathons,	__student council
selling chances)	__honor society
__school newspaper	__intramural sports
__interscholastic sports	

	Yes	No
A process exists to evaluate annually each student activity.	☐	☐
The principal meets with an umbrella group of student leaders monthly.	☐	☐
The school has an affiliate school and the two schools are engaged in a variety of enriching (academic bowl, art exhibits, pen pal or other joint writing project) and school spirit (basketball, lacrosse, softball competitions) activities.	☐	☐

Caring

Reflective Practice Exercise #4

SUSTAINING CARING (STUDENTS)

Determine whether or not the statements that follow accurately reflect your school's level of caring. For those statements you find do not reflect what your school is currently doing, undertake an action plan in concert with your governing team to increase your school's caring quotient.

Goal: To promote and maintain a strong respectful relationship with the student body.

	Yes	No
Every discipline has students who participate in local, state, and national contests/competitions.	☐	☐
Conflict resolution and peer mediation programs are embedded in the school's curriculum.	☐	☐
A student tutoring club exists (e.g., honor society, volunteers).	☐	☐
The student council, honor society, and student newspaper leadership input is validated via implementation of their suggestions to make the entire school program more effective.	☐	☐
Home visits are made.	☐	☐
Prevention, intervention, apprehension, and counseling programs are available to combat possession of weapons and violent acts.	☐	☐
Assistant principals organize and meet with grade-level team leaders monthly.	☐	☐
The principal meets with the student umbrella leadership group monthly.	☐	☐

Caring

Reflective Practice Exercise #5

INITIATING CARING (ADULTS)

Determine whether or not the statements that follow accurately reflect your school's level of caring. For those statements you find do not reflect what your school is currently doing, undertake an action plan in concert with your governing team to increase your school's caring quotient.

Goal: To establish a school climate that reflects the school's mission and provides an atmosphere that is conducive to learning.

	Yes	No
The principal is visible—greeting, monitoring, and providing support by walking around the entire school at least twice daily.	☐	☐
An annual goal-setting conference is held with each professional and classified staff member.	☐	☐
The principal attends each department and/or team meeting at least once during the course of the academic school year.	☐	☐
School administrators recognize each staff member's birthday.	☐	☐
There is a functioning school hospitality committee.	☐	☐
School administrators are in attendance at programs recognizing students' achievements and/or showcasing their talents.	☐	☐
A school fund exists to support teacher professional development.	☐	☐
Teacher input is solicited for teaching assignment preferences.	☐	☐
Partnership exists with social service agencies, juvenile justice departments, and advocacy groups to address student needs that the school is not equipped to address.	☐	☐
Support staff are encouraged to have relationships with representatives of social service agencies.	☐	☐
The employee assistance program is used to address staff personnel issues and needs.	☐	☐

Caring

Reflective Practice Exercise #6

STABILIZING CARING (ADULTS)

Determine whether or not the statements that follow accurately reflect your school's level of caring. For those statements you find do not reflect what your school is currently doing, undertake an action plan in concert with your governing team to increase your school's caring quotient.

GOAL: To establish a school climate that reflects the school's mission and provides an atmosphere that is conducive to learning.

	Yes	No
Students are informed, in a timely fashion, when they are in danger of failing.	☐	☐
Counselors conduct individual counseling, group counseling, group guidance classes, and academic advisement sessions.	☐	☐

Parental contact includes (check all that apply):

__back to school night	__PTA/PTSO meetings	__volunteer programs
__parent workshops	__parents as guest speakers	__class visitors
__handbooks	__home visits	__invitations to school
__telephone calls	__letters from teachers	__programs and activities
__parent/teacher conferences	and/or progress reports	__parent caller machine
	__course outlines mailed as needed	__newsletters

	Yes	No
A system exists by which students may appeal, within the school, teachers' and assistant principals' decisions affecting the students adversely.	☐	☐
Students' work is posted in every classroom. (100% means every classroom.)	☐	☐
Fairs (academic/vocational/unified arts) are held annually to display student work that has been judged as exceeding minimal expectations.	☐	☐
Recognition programs are held to salute students' exceptional athletic, academic, community service, and comportment achievements.	☐	☐
Midyear goal status conferences are conducted with all staff.	☐	☐
School administrators commend teachers and other staff (cafeteria workers, bus drivers, teachers' aides, and other professionals), verbally and in writing (memos, daily bulletin, cards, notes, public address system, announcements near the sign-in sheet), for their cooperation and leadership for schoolwide goals attainment.	☐	☐
National Teachers Week is observed in the school.	☐	☐
Students' input is sought through the use of surveys and focus groups, at the completion of instruction units, etc., and is used for improving school climate.	☐	☐

Caring

Reflective Practice Exercise #7

SUSTAINING CARING (ADULTS)

Determine whether or not the statements that follow accurately reflect your school's level of caring. For those statements you find do not reflect what your school is currently doing, undertake an action plan in concert with your governing team to increase your school's caring quotient.

Goal: To establish a school climate that reflects the school's mission and provides an atmosphere that is conducive to learning.

	Yes	No
The guidance department administers "students helping students" programs (e.g., peer facilitators, peer mediation).	☐	☐
Programs to enhance students' self-esteem (e.g., Student of the Month, kudos for helpers, advisory, mentoring, adopt-a-student) are definable and defensible and not limited to nonachievers.	☐	☐
Contact is made with parents/guardians when students achieve as well as when the students' behavior is unacceptable.	☐	☐

3

Change

Leading in a New Direction

Being intentional is critical to sustaining change. The principal of Woodson Junior High was continuously heard to say, "School is not a place for adult conveniences (giving grades, focusing on barriers and stereotypes, not teaching to students' learning styles, blaming the victim). No! School is a safe, intellectually stimulating and validating social institution for children and youth."

Every six weeks teachers conferred with the principal about student grades and the strategies they had used for reflection about grades.

"If Hector is failing your course, it's your fault," the principal would say to a teacher. "How are you reteaching content? Are you using alternative assessments and guided practice to give Hector every opportunity to learn and to show what he knows?"

These conferences set a tone in the school that said, "Data drive instructional planning and execution, and it's okay not to have all the answers!"

■ RESPONDING TO FORCES OF CHANGE

There is a fundamental duality to our response to change: We both embrace and resist it. Moreover, change means something different to each and every individual. The key factor in change is what it means to those who must implement it and that its primary meanings encourage resistance. Evans (1996) gives us the following common responses to change:

- It provokes loss.
- It challenges competence.
- It creates confusion.
- It causes conflict.

■ TAKING CHARGE OF CHANGE

People resist change in the following situations:

- It takes them by surprise.
- It is forced on them and they are told rather than asked.
- It upsets their comfort zone, familiar habits, and routines.
- They don't feel competent.
- They don't feel they're in control.
- They don't understand the reason or benefit.
- It creates more work.

Getting others involved in implementation can mitigate some of this resistance. Try the following:

- Make them feel a part of the change.
- Tell them about changes and decisions that will interest them or affect them.
- Share your plans with them.
- Tell them why.
- Ask or invite them to help rather than telling them.
- Ask for their ideas on other goals, on things to correct or improve.
- Get their ideas on action steps, ways to measure, obstacles, and solutions.

What are the forces that are changing the nature of the principalship generally, and the urban principalship specifically? Where are they coming from? Are they new and different from the forces that shaped the schools of yesterday? How are they affecting schools?

According to Goldring and Rallis (2000), five forces exist that help shape a principal's behavior:

> **Unlocking Intentional Action for Sustained Change**
>
> Carefully review the scenario presented at the beginning of this chapter. What are your feelings about how the principal held the teacher responsible for a student's failure? Have you ever acted in a similar manner? What were the results? If you haven't acted that way, what do you think would be the response of your staff if you did? What is the point at which being intentional becomes being belligerent?

- Teachers are becoming teacher-leaders.
- Parents are more vocal and action-oriented advocates.
- Student bodies are more diverse with a variety of needs.
- The social and technological contexts of schools are more complex.
- State and federal reform mandates are setting priorities. (p. 5)

They conclude that recognizing and acknowledging these forces is the first step to leading a dynamic school. The principal has several options in dealing with the forces: The principal can ignore them—to the peril of the school; the principal can react to them—allowing them to drive the school; or the principal can take charge—using them to shape a dynamic school (Goldring & Rallis, 2000, p. 6).

As alluded to in the Introduction, a study group of faculty and staff at four schools of education within the University of California system focused on urban school districts in an unpublished paper. They use more descriptive language to note factors similar to those described by Goldring and Rallis. According to the study group, urban school districts face the following challenges:

1. Some students' value of schooling may be ambivalent, resulting in inconsistent engagement in academic and cocurricular activities. Such ambivalence may be the result of parents who have modest levels of schooling or who come from countries with different schooling traditions.

2. Some students often fall behind grade-level expectations, and then parents and district and state officials exert pressure to improve their performance and help them keep up with their peers.

3. Language issues are complex and usually include students from many different language groups as well as students who come to school unversed in Standard English.

4. The racial and ethnic diversity of urban schools creates another set of distinctive issues, sometimes reflected in conflicts among students, sometimes in misunderstandings between faculties and students or between educators and parents.

5. High levels of poverty often lead to children lacking the kinds of financial and parental support that children need to focus on learning.

6. The institutional practices that have developed in many school districts often limit and constrain educational opportunities for urban students rather than expand and enrich them.

7. Urban children may suffer more than others from being in anonymous settings where no one knows them well.

8. Urban neighborhoods are often turbulent places.

9. The teaching force is often inexperienced and untrained, hired with emergency credentials or training in special, short programs. Teacher training programs often fail to prepare teachers for the particular characteristics of urban schools.

10. Resources in urban schools and districts often seem to be stretched thin.

What neither of these reports cites explicitly is the impact of teachers' beliefs about their own efficacy and the tenure of urban superintendents in the school districts. There is a body of research (Bandura, 1986, 1993, 1996, 1997) about teacher self-efficacy and the lack thereof results in poor performance and nonattainment of goals. Lack of stability in the top leadership in a school district contributes to widespread lack of focus on student achievement and ineffective use of existing resources.

The lists are daunting. Where does the urban school principal begin? After recognizing and acknowledging these forces exist, the principal has several options in dealing with the forces:

- Ignore them—to the peril of the school.
- React to them—allowing them to drive the school.
- Take charge—using them to shape a dynamic school.

Contemporary scholars have observed an emerging style of principal leadership characterized by high faculty involvement in and ownership of decisions, management of the school's vision, and an emphasis on significant change and improvement. New terminology was needed to describe the evolution of the principalship in the face of school restructuring, school-based decision making, and teacher empowerment. Conley and Goldman (1994) use the term "facilitative leadership" to describe how principals come to lead without dominating in this new environment.

■ PLANNING FOR AND BRINGING ABOUT CHANGE

In their research on organizational change as it relates to school reform, Michael Curtis and Stephanie Stollar (1996) identify interpersonal relationships, planning, and problem-solving skills as key components of effective organizational change. They present a six-step model for principals to use:

1. Describe the problem and identify the desired outcome.

2. Identify facilitators and inhibitors to the change process.

3. Select an obstacle.

4. Brainstorm resources and activities to address the obstacle.

5. Design a plan of action with accountability.

6. Establish a procedure for follow-up and revision.

Michael Fullan (1993) contends that educational reform requires interrelated changes in schools and teachers characterized by restructuring (changing teachers' roles), reculturing (changing the culture of schools so that teachers work collaboratively in a professional community), and retiming (altering the relative time teachers spend in preparation and instruction). Much can be learned during the change process by all parties involved. Perhaps learning that conflict helps bring about change is the most difficult for a leader to process. However, it is the dynamic tensions created by the machinations of conflict that power change. As Fullan (1993) puts it, "Problems are our friends . . . successful organizations don't have fewer problems, they just solve more problems" (p. 23). Organizations that address problems and connect to the wider environment to collaboratively solve them are the most successful. Continuing professional development must be tied to widening the role of teachers and altering the conditions under which teachers work.

Change Takes Time

Conventional wisdom says that everyone wants progress but no one wants change. Something as simple as changing a habit is never a quick, easy process. People who have tried to stop smoking or to change their eating habits know how difficult this is! Those of us who have changed jobs and homes also can speak about the difficulty of adapting to change. Research shows that different people accept change at different rates and some never adapt to change. People fear change. Put simply, they fear the unknown. They fear failure. They fear commitment. They fear disapproval. They fear success.

> ### Unlocking Efficacy
>
> Before we focus on selective research about school change, it is important that you examine data on one classroom in your school to determine what factors—risk and protective—affect selected students, and data on one teacher's sense of efficacy as regards the difference he or she can make in spite of the factors. This information will provide you with a personal perspective of the magnitude of the challenge you face in your new assignment. See Reflective Practice Exercise #1.

CONCERNS-BASED ADOPTION MODEL ■

For some time, researchers have been interested in the concerns of teachers and how these concerns focus their attention on a limited range of issues relating to change. At the University of Texas, this work led to the development of the Concerns-Based Adoption Model (CBAM), which describes the changing feelings of people as they learn about a proposed change, prepare to use it, use it, and modify it as a result. The model proposes seven stages of concerns (Hall & Loucks, 1978):

1.	Awareness	I am not concerned about it.
2.	Informational	I would like to know more about it.
3.	Personal	How will using it affect me?
4.	Management	I seem to be spending all my time getting material ready.
5.	Consequence	How is my use affecting kids?
6.	Collaboration	I am concerned about relating what I am doing to what other teachers are doing.
7.	Refocusing	I have some ideas about something that would work even better.

Unlocking Positive Attitudes About Change

One's mindset is critical when thinking about change. As noted in Table 3.1, it is possible to think positively about change. Frequently, the first words that come to mind when thinking about change are negative. People are comfortable with the familiar and fear the unknown, often with good reason. Still, herein, we focus on the positive. How many additional positive words can you list as you think about change? When introducing a change in your school, conduct a brainstorming activity that requires participants to list only positive or neutral words concerning the proposed change. Or, you could simply allow them to list all the words they can think of. Then place the words in the three categories. If the list of positive words is the shortest, ask the group to add additional positive words to the list. Conduct a discussion about the choice of words. Don't ignore the downside; just try to find a balance. Ask the faculty and staff this question: How does language affect change outcomes?

Table 3.1   Thinking Positively About Change

Negative words	Neutral words	Positive words
fight	tension	fun
battle	problem	excitement
war	people	challenge
argument	discussion	opportunity

Although not every teacher might experience the stages in the linear fashion presented, the stages do represent a general kind of development that takes place as changes are adopted and used continuously.

■ CONSENSUS-BASED ADOPTION MODEL

Leaders and planners need to decide who must be committed to the change and how to reach these key people. Do not underestimate the importance of having a critical mass to assist with the innovation. A critical mass is *the right number of the right people.* People who work together have varying degrees of power and influence in the organization. For any school initiative to succeed, the principal must bring together the most powerful people to plan and execute tasks. The key to success is a respectful representation of all points of view—even those not in harmony with the administration.

Remember, it will be difficult for an entire school staff to reach consensus on both the need for change and the type of change needed. Furthermore, if consensus is reached in the early stages, it may be more on doing things to increase job satisfaction than on fostering high achievement among all students.

■ OVERCOMING RESISTANCE TO CHANGE

Two approaches to overcoming resistance to change are provided for your consideration.

Approach #1

Approach #1 is advocated by Burt Nanus, Professor of Management and Organization and Director of Research in the University of California's Leadership Institute.

1. You can implement the new vision deliberately, making sure everyone understands the new direction and introducing the least disruptive or threatening changes first.

2. You can avoid resistance by isolating the departments/grade levels/teams responsible for pioneering the new direction from the existing organization until they prove their worth or acquire legitimacy and acceptance. This is called conducting a pilot study.

3. You can put the new thrust in the hands of younger people with less commitment to the status quo and extend it later to other parts of the organization. Or, you can assign responsibilities to opinion leaders and champions in the organization who know how to take advantage of informal networks to establish a sense of renewal and progress with the new vision.

4. You can foster a culture that embraces change and innovation so that the new vision is not seen as something unusual but rather as part of the continuing evolution of your organization. (Nanus, 1994)

Unlocking the Power of Critical Mass

If you are newly assigned to the school, you will need the help of teachers and other staff members. Suggested activities for identifying and using a critical mass follow.

- Ask staff members to identify colleagues on whom they would depend
  - in an emergency
  - for specialized help
  - as an advocate
  - if they needed a confidant

- Analyze the names, and note the names that appear most frequently.
- Develop a staff sociogram. Record who talks with whom most often and who is closest to whom. What are the cliques?
- Design a school organization chart depicting by size the names of the most influential and potent people.
- Carefully observe staff members who seem to be most respected by colleagues, students, and community leaders.

Box 3.1 Overview of the Concerns-Based Adoption Model

- Change takes time and persistence.
- Individuals go through stages in the change process and have different needs at different stages.
- Change strategies are most effective when they are chosen to meet people's needs.
- Administrative support and approval are needed for change to occur.
- Developing a critical mass of support is just as important as developing administrative support.
- An individual or committee must take responsibility for organizing and managing the change.
- The objective is to benefit students, not just "convert" staff.
- Successful change is planned and managed.

Approach #2

Approach #2 is advocated by the National Association of Secondary School Principals.

1. Consider who gains and loses from change.

2. Anticipate unfavorable reactions and minimize their impact.

3. Divert and diffuse unneeded conflict.

4. Invite private feedback from critics, especially blockers and naysayers.

5. Meet people's four basic work needs:

   - need for clear expectations,
   - need for future certainty,
   - need for social interaction,
   - need for control over environment.

6. Encourage innovations and change with the potential to achieve mutually desired goals.

7. Do not impose solutions on people.

8. Emphasize open involvement and commitment.

9. Focus on what people think is immediately important and troublesome.

■ STUDY CIRCLES: FABLES

The intention of this chapter has been to provide content and Reflective Practice Exercises that will cause you to think about change in a new way. Sometimes, however, a simple story is more instructive and memorable. In this spirit, consider reading two books about change: *The Eagle and the Monk* (1997) by William A. Jenkins and Richard W. Oliver and *Who Moved My Cheese?* (1998) by Spencer Johnson, M.D. You might also consider buying copies of the books for your assistant principals and instructional leadership council. The books are ideal for study circles to read prior to implementing a major change in your school.

In *The Eagle and the Monk,* a fable is used to present nine principles of successful change:

- Accept your worth.
- Acknowledge others' worth.
- Generate trust, learn by empathy.
- Embrace change.
- Unleash the synergy.
- Discover champions.
- Depend on masters.
- Find a sage.
- Liberate decision making.

To stimulate dialogue about the fable, the authors include definitions of each principle with accompanying generalizations, thought-provoking questions to be discussed in pairs or groups, and passages from each chapter about the chapter's respective principle of change. The reader becomes conversant with The Rock, The Island, The Wind, The Nest, The Sage, The Wall, and The Tree as change principles in a way that doesn't allow the reader to put up learning barriers.

Who Moved My Cheese? "is a story about change that takes place in a maze where four amusing characters look for cheese. Cheese is a metaphor for what we want to have in life, whether it is a job, a relationship, money, a big house, freedom, health, recognition, spiritual peace, or even an activity like jogging or golf" (Johnson, 1998, p. 14).

The book contains three sections. In the first, "A Gathering," former classmates talk at a class reunion about trying to deal with the changes happening in their lives. The second section, the core of the book, is "The Story of Who Moved My Cheese?" In the third section, "A Discussion," people discuss what the story meant to them and how they are going to use it in their work and in their lives.

As an urban school principal taking charge of change, it is imperative that you keep one thing in mind: People resist change when they are not involved, so you need to get them involved!

CHANGE REFLECTIVE PRACTICE EXERCISES

Change

Reflective Practice Exercise #1

Select a teacher's class in which there is modest academic, social, and behavioral student success due to the teacher's efforts and the positive school climate. Randomly select five boys and girls from the class. Your task is to identify risk and protective factors in the students' families, in the community, among their peers, and in the school.

The students' family information should be broad based. Review the students' school records to note their racial and ethnic backgrounds, socioeconomic status, family mobility (the number of times the students' families have moved since being enrolled in school), their attendance, and their academic achievement based on grades (teacher assessment) and standardized tests. Supplement this information by interviewing the teacher and/or the students.

1. Develop a profile of each student. Note similarities and differences among the students. Some questions to facilitate your completion of this task follow:

   a. How many students

      - live in two-parent (male/female) families?
      - live with one parent?
      - live with one or more grandparents?
      - are wards of the state (e.g., are in foster care or in a juvenile group home)?
      - have one parent incarcerated?
      - live in blended families (e.g., families in which one parent is a stepparent)?
      - are emancipated young adults (e.g., have reached majority age and are living on their own)?
      - are the children of a teenage parent (e.g., one parent is 17 years of age or younger)?
      - are in families that are bilingual?

   b. How many students have been retained once? Twice?
   c. What has been the children's family mobility? How many students have had two or more addresses in any one year of schooling?
   d. How many students' parents are pursuing higher education or upgrading their skills for better employment?
   e. How many of the students live in large families (five or more children)?
   f. How many students are responsible for taking care of their siblings?
   g. How many students participate in some type of religious activity on a regular basis?

2. Examine the students' significant relationships with peers in the classroom and outside the classroom. Are there strong friendships? Is any student isolated? Do the students get along well with each other?

3. List the first three words that come to your mind about the community in which the students live. If you have no knowledge about the students' neighborhoods, visit at least four streets the students live on before you complete the remainder of this reflective exercise. Describe the immediate community in which the students live. Who are the role models in the community? Are intergenerational ties evident in the community? What are the external support systems for students and their families within a 10-block radius of the school?

4. Now think about the three types of climate in your school that affect students directly: academic, physical, and social-emotional. For each climate, list two ways that these climates nurture and support students' growth.

5. Use the chart in Figure 3.1 to record your analysis of the information you have about the students. Note: for every risk factor you list, you must list a protective one. This will require you to reflect deeply about positives in the students' families, the community, and the school environment. As the school leader, your role now becomes one of "accentuating the positive."

Figure 3.1

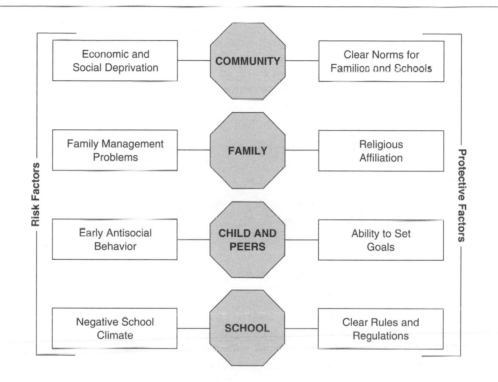

6. Interview the teacher using the Efficacy Scale in Form 3.1. Have a conversation with the teacher about your analysis and about how the two of you might partner—to accelerate students' academic achievement and their social development, to involve their parents, and to involve neighborhood agencies in the school. Prior to this conversation, develop a one-page statement addressing the following. (This statement will be used to guide your conversation with the teacher. Remember to applaud the teacher for what he or she is already doing prior to making the suggestions.)

   a. Accentuate the strengths of students' families and their neighborhoods.
   b. Reinforce students' interests through the four academic disciplines.
   c. Use students' address information and neighborhood agencies information to teach a mathematics lesson or a lesson in some other subject.

Form 3.1   Hoy and Woolfolk's Short Form of the Teacher Efficacy Scale

The statements about organizations, people, and teaching presented below can determine your attitudes as an educator. There are no correct or incorrect answers. We are interested only in your frank opinions. Your responses will remain confidential. **Instructions:** Please indicate your personal opinion about each statement by circling the appropriate response at the right of each statement.

Key: 1 = strongly agree, 2 =moderately agree, 3 = agree slightly more than disagree, 4 = disagree slightly more than agree, 5 = moderately disagree, 6 = strongly disagree.

1. The amount a student can learn is primarily related to family background.   1 2 3 4 5 6

2. If students are not disciplined at home, they aren't likely to accept any discipline.   1 2 3 4 5 6

3. When I really try, I can get through to most difficult students.   1 2 3 4 5 6

4. A teacher is very much limited in what he or she can achieve because a student's home environment is a large influence on his or her achievement.   1 2 3 4 5 6

5. If parents would do more for their children, I could do more.   1 2 3 4 5 6

6. If a student did not remember information I gave in a previous lesson, I would know how to increase his or her retention in the next lesson.   1 2 3 4 5 6

7. If a student in my class becomes disruptive and noisy, I feel assured that I know some techniques to redirect him or her quickly.   1 2 3 4 5 6

8. If one of my students couldn't do a class assignment, I would be able to accurately assess whether the assignment was at the correct level of difficulty.   1 2 3 4 5 6

9. If I really try hard, I can get through to even the most difficult or unmotivated students.   1 2 3 4 5 6

10. When it comes right down to it, a teacher really can't do much because most of a student's motivation and performance depends on his or her home environment.   1 2 3 4 5 6

SOURCE: Hoy, W. K., Woolfolk, A. E., "Teachers' Sense of Efficacy and the Organizational Health of Schools," *Elementary School Journal,* 93:4 (1993) pp. 356–372. Used with permission of University of Chicago Press.

Change

Reflective Practice Exercise #2

How ready are you for change? Assess your personal readiness for change by completing the following.

1. In which of the following topic areas do you most want to concentrate your change effort? (Circle one or more.)

      Curriculum Alignment

      Instructional Strategies

      Use of Time and Organization

      Leadership Challenges

      Assessment

2. What is your specific change area?

3. Assess yourself in the following areas (1 being "Needs lots of work" and 5 being "Taken care of").

   a. Assessment of Myself, the Climate, Stages of Concern, Commitment, and Resources

        1   2   3   4   5

   b. Clarification of the Vision, Beliefs, the Purpose of Change, Tasks, and Parameters of the Change

        1   2   3   4   5

   c. Involvement and facilitation through Development of Site-Based Decision Making, Development of Group Process Skills, Development of Community of Learners, Skills to Deal With Conflict

        1   2   3   4   5

   d. Monitoring and feedback by Evaluation of the Project, Evaluation of the Process, Reassessment of the Stages of Concern, the Process of Change

        1   2   3   4   5

Change

Reflective Practice Exercise #3

1. Think about the three most recent changes your immediate supervisor directed principals to follow. Review the adopter descriptions below and identify which adopter type you were in response to the changes. Surprises? If so, why? If not, why not? Write a paragraph assessing your behavior.

   Now think about a recent change in your personal life. Which adopter type were you? Why? Reflect on this choice. Compare your personal life choice to the work environment choices. What were the similarities? What were the differences?

2. If you have recently implemented a schoolwide change, place each staff member's name under one of the adopter categories on the roster. Did you get a critical mass that resulted in successful implementation of the change initiative? If your answer is no, share the results with your leadership team and discuss how knowledge and use of the above might have assisted you with your change initiative.

ADOPTER GROUPING IN THE CONCERNS-BASED ADOPTION MODEL

The Concerns-Based Adoption Model proposes that the leader consider the following groupings of adopters and their typical percentages as worthy of attention when initiating a given change.

Innovator: eager to try new ideas, open to change, and willing to take risks; usually perceived as naïve or a little crazy and, therefore, not well-integrated into the social structure (8%).

Leader: open to change, but more thoughtful about getting involved; trusted by other staff and sought for advice and opinion (17%).

Early Majority: cautious and deliberate about deciding to adopt an innovation; tends to be a follower, not a leader (29%).

Late Majority: skeptical of adopting new ideas and "set in their ways"; can be won over by a combination of peer pressure and administrative expectations (29%).

Resister: suspicious and generally opposed to new ideas; usually low in influence and often isolated from the mainstream (17%).

These percentages illustrate that any idea (including changes in curriculum alignment, use of time and organization, teaching, school environment, testing, bus schedules) takes time to catch on, and it won't be universally accepted. Proponents suggest that one recognize this fact and concentrate efforts on those who will or might agree with you.

4

Charisma

Leading With Personality

The principal of a large urban middle school in the inner city always dresses up when she addresses a parent group or student assembly. Knowing the power of a grand entrance, she waits until everyone is seated before coming into the meeting. She enters the room smiling and clapping her hands. Walking boldly around the room, she gets the audience to join in the clapping. After the rhythm is going well, she raises a finger for the clapping to stop. She says,

"Stand up. Look at your neighbor and repeat after me, 'Neighbor, I am a winner. You are a winner. Everyone in this room is a winner. Today is a great day. We support and love each other. Reaching our goal is possible. I say reaching our goal is possible.' Clap your hands. Give your partner a high five and say, 'Yeah!'"

By using her charm and charisma, she connects with the audience. They are ready to listen to her message or attend to her requests. When the meeting is over, members of adult audiences usually want to, in black church lingo, "touch the flesh" before saying good-bye. People in the audience stand in line to say goodbye or good night to the principal.

■ IT'S A BIG JOB, AND YOU'RE THE ONE WHO CAN DO IT

Being a principal is a "big" job that requires some high-level skills. Figure 4.1 is a fictitious ad for a school principal that appeared in *Education Week,* in an article titled "Getting Real About Leadership" (Evans, 1995). Although tongue in cheek, the job description does cause one to pause. Next, consider a list of roles that describe the principal. There are some very specific abilities and skills we want principals to possess, such as the following:

> **Unlocking an Accurate Job Description for the Urban School Principal**
>
> Contemplate the ad for a principal from *Education Week* (Figure 4.1). To what extent does it mirror the expectations you face as an urban school principal? How would you rewrite the ad to advertise for your job?

- The ability to keep and dispense information
- Trustworthiness
- Flexibility
- Comfort with risk taking
- The ability to listen well and hold confidences
- The ability to lead, negotiate, support, and evaluate

Figure 4.1   An Ad for a Principal

> Wanted: A miracle worker who can do more with less, pacify rival groups, endure chronic second guessing, tolerate low levels of support, process large volumes of paper and work double shifts (75 nights a year). He or she will have carte blanche to innovate but cannot spend much money, replace any personnel, or upset any constituency.

SOURCE: Evans (1995). Reprinted with permission of Human Relations Service, Inc.

■ THE PRINCIPALSHIP IN ITS CONTEMPORARY CONTEXT

Michael Fullan (1998) points out that the job of the principal has become increasingly complex and constrained. Principals find themselves locked in with less and less room to maneuver. Consider the following situations as they relate to the urban school.

Meeting Expectations for Student Progress

Some students in urban schools often fall behind grade-level expectations. Then parents, districts, and state officials exert pressure to improve student performance and help them keep up with their peers. Certain solutions—ending social promotion, requiring exit exams, and adding programs that use a remedial pedagogy—are frequently less effective than other kinds of enrichment activities that both intensify instruction and change pedagogical practices. Unfortunately, the urban principal does not have the option to institute such alternatives.

Poverty

High levels of poverty often cause children to lack the kinds of financial and parental support they need to focus on learning. Urban principals are forced to consider developing, in partnership with others, such programs as these: health programs, nutrition programs, child care and after-school programs, in-house juvenile justice probation programs, and other support services programs.

Limiting Educational Opportunities

Some institutional practices limit educational opportunities. Such practices include the following:

- Tracking
- Retention in grade
- Placement in special education
- Disciplinary proceedings that banish students from school
- Norm-referenced tests used as gatekeepers
- Programs following remedial pedagogies

Mandates Related to Discipline

In the past, parents who complained that their child was being harassed or picked on heard the behavior described as teasing. A remedy would have consisted of a talk with the principal or school counselor. "Playing the dozen" (a quick exchange of clever insults) and teasing are common ways of communicating in urban schools. State law and school policies require that the urban school principal follow a prescribed, investigative process that could take days to complete. Valuable time that could have been given to instructional issues is now lost.

Cultural and Community Norms in Conflict With State Laws

Minority parents' preferred discipline tactics of spanking and verbally reprimanding their children, with support from the principal for doing just that, are now a violation of the law. Community expectations are that parents will engage in conversations with children about their inappropriate behavior rather than correct them with physical contact. Moreover, it is not uncommon for urban children to call 911 to report their parents for child abuse when they are angry with their parents.

Union Rules

Teachers' union contracts stipulate that students cannot be readmitted to a teacher's class without a satisfactory conference with the teacher. Such agreements do not take into consideration the urban principal's busy schedule or teachers who have poor classroom management skills that contribute to student disruptions.

At the very time that proactive leadership is essential, urban principals are in the least favorable position to provide it. They need a new mindset and guidelines for action to make a difference in their schools.

■ CHARISMA BY ANY OTHER NAME

The word *charisma* is of Greek origin, literally meaning a gift, and it was originally identified as a gift of grace or divinely inspired calling to service, office, or leadership. Today the term has entered common usage in a variety of forms and is widely applied to virtually every situation in which a popular public or political personality is involved. There are three ways charisma is normally defined today.

The Classic Interpretation

The classical philosophers saw charisma as a supernatural endowment. A leader derives his or her charisma from divine gifts and maintains this power as long as followers believe in his or her extraordinary qualities.

Awe Inspiring

Here charisma is expanded to refer to the sacred or awe-inspiring property of groups, offices, and even objects.

Personality

Charisma is popularly used to refer to the personal qualities or to the presence of a political leader.

Followers attribute authority to charismatic leaders through their faith and belief in them and in their mission. Charismatic authority *in organizations* involves an interaction of leader, followers, and moral order; in the eyes of the followers, the leader personifies that order. True charismatic leaders are able to place themselves and their mission beyond the realm of the ordinary and thus extract extraordinary effort, dedication, and faith from followers.

■ HEROIC LEADERSHIP

James MacGregor Burns concludes that the concept of charisma has fertilized the study of leadership. Charisma, for MacGregor Burns (1982), takes on the following overlapping meanings:

- A leader's magical qualities
- An emotional bond between leader and led
- Dependence on a father figure by the masses
- Popular assumption that a leader is powerful, omniscient, and virtuous

- Imputation of enormous supernatural power to leaders (or secular power, or both)
- Popular support for a leader that verges on love

SOURCE: Excerpts on charisma and heroic leadership from *Leadership* by James MacGregor Burns. Copyright © 1978 by James MacGregor Burns. Reprinted with permission of HarperCollins Publishers.

CHARISMATIC LEADERS ■

The term *charismatic* is seldom used to describe education leaders. It is more frequently applied to political, religious, and business leaders. Yet, education leaders are just as numerous, and they attract equally large numbers of followers. Four immediately come to mind. The first is Horace Mann, considered the father of the American public school because he worked to increase the availability and quality of free, nondenominational public schools. Next is John Dewey, father of progressive education, who advocated learning by doing and teaching the child, not the subject. Third is William H. McGuffey, who wrote a series of books commonly known as *McGuffey's Readers*, designed to teach reading to school children. And last is Noah Webster, an educator and author of the late eighteenth and early nineteenth centuries, best known for his *American Dictionary of the English Language* and *Blue-Backed Speller*. Webster worked for the establishment of a distinctive American version of the English language; for example, he insisted on such spellings as wagon, center, and honor in place of the standard British waggon, centre, and honour. A number of widely used dictionaries, of varying scope and quality, still bear Webster's name.

African American educators who have influenced many an urban educator's practice include Booker T. Washington, Mary McLeod Bethune, Carter G. Woodson, Dr. Ron Edmonds, Dr. Benjamin Mays, and Marva Collins. Booker T. Washington headed Tuskegee Institute, an African American college in Alabama. The best known of his many books is *Up From Slavery*, which describes his heroic achievement of learning to read and write. Mary McLeod Bethune, large in stature and charming in manner, founded a school for girls that later became part of Bethune-Cookman College. Mrs. Bethune promoted the teaching of black history in the public schools.

Unlocking the Power Potential of Charisma

Consider the various traits of a successful school leader introduced so far. Roll these traits, attributes, abilities, and skills into a lovely ball of multicolored yarns, and you get a sum that is greater than its component parts. In leadership, that "something" becomes charisma—a tangible, yet intangible something that makes us remember, revere, gravitate towards, and support the leader.

What do you think this chapter's subtitle, "Leading with Personality," means? Might it have an alternative meaning?

Unlocking Lessons Learned From Leaders

What leaders in what fields have influenced your practice as an educator and leader? What qualities did they possess that you admire?

For an in-depth study of leaders in various fields, turn to the Charisma Reflective Practice Exercises at the end of this chapter.

Carter G. Woodson, educator extraordinaire, is considered the father of black history because of his insistence that facts and information about blacks be codified in encyclopedias and books. He also started Black History Week, which has since become Black History Month. Marva Collins, in her West Side Preparatory School in Chicago, affirmed that the problems that confront our public schools are not insoluble. Ms. Collins taught nonreaders how to read well using Shakespeare. Dr. Ron Edmonds and Dr. Benjamin Mays were educators who had tremendous influence on students and peers (as superintendents and college presidents). Their insights and research about effective education strategies for African Americans are quoted widely.

■ FOLLOWING THE LEADER

MacGregor Burns (1982) uses the term *heroic leadership.* He underscores the importance of the type of relationship between the leader and the led. Heroic leadership is thus defined as follows:

- Belief in leaders because of their personage alone, aside from their tested capacities, experience, or stand on issues
- Faith in the leaders' capacity to overcome obstacles and crises
- Readiness to grant leaders the power to handle crises
- Mass support for such leaders expressed directly—through votes, applause, letters, shaking hands—rather than through intermediaries or institutions

An Ongoing Difference of Opinion

Social scientists who study leaders' characteristics frequently come to different conclusions about representative traits of charismatic leaders. The following traits, however, appear on most lists:

- Intelligence
- Self-assurance
- Enthusiasm
- Good health
- Initiative
- Sociability

Situational Theories of Leadership

Critics of the "trait approach" point to the unwieldy nature of the above list and to the widely varied characteristics it contains to substantiate their claim that there is no "essence of leadership" that will hold for all cases. After World War II, the "essence of leadership" approach was abandoned in favor of situational theories. Situational theories postulate that leader styles or behaviors may change radically from one setting to another. *Situationists* believe that a person who is a leader in one situation may be a follower in another; traits useful in one situation may actually be disastrous in others. Hence, leaders are not born with any particular traits that determine leadership. Situationists have less interest in what a leader is than in what he or she does in a given situation (Smith & Piele, 2006). This is especially true for urban school leaders.

Consider the leadership skill of decisiveness. If there is one characteristic that adults of poverty respect in urban school principals, it is decisiveness. When a parent comes to the school because of a gang fight, a teacher being disrespectful to his son or daughter, or his child's failure in school, he does not expect to leave the conference with the administrator with a list of options to consider and bring back to a second conference. He expects definitive solutions to the problem. For example, for a gang fight, the parent of a student attending an urban school (1) wants to know the names of all students involved and (2) demands that all students involved receive the same punishment. If not satisfied that all students will receive the same punishment, this parent will call the principal unfair and contact the principal's supervisor. In a suburban school, just the opposite happens and is usually expected. The parent wants to know the range of options for punishment and whether or not the punishment has to be served now or can be served at a later date. The upper-income parent wants a unique consequence for his child. If the principal is not flexible (i.e., is decisive) regarding this expectation, then the parent's lawyer becomes involved. Litigation or the threat of litigation ensues. A second conference is expected.

Smith and Piele (2006) point out that it may be a bit premature to throw out trait research. Citing Edwin Locke, they assert that "it now seems clear that certain traits and motives do indeed influence a leader's effectiveness" (p. 16). They conclude that the difficulty is that certain traits are necessary, but not sufficient, for effective leadership; that is, they work in combination with other factors. Summarizing significant findings of trait research as well as more recent research on educational leaders, Smith and Piele paint a portrait of an effective leader (see Figure 4.2).

Effective leaders have energy and involvement, competence (intelligence, technical knowledge and skill, interpersonal competence), personality (sociability, psychological health, charisma), and character.

Unlocking the Origin of Your Leadership Skills

If leaders do have traits and characteristics that separate them from followers, where do the traits come from? Some, like intelligence, come from a poorly understood combination of genetic endowment and early nurturing. Others, like cooperativeness and ease in groups, are believed to spring chiefly from parental influences. Many specific leadership skills are obviously learned through experience (Smith & Piele 2006, p. 30). Think about the exceptional skills you possess. Of these three sources, what is the origin of most of your leadership skills?

Unlocking the Successful Organizational Leadership

As the organizational leader of an urban school, consider three options outlined by Sergiovanni: boss, messiah, and administrator (1990b, p. 150). The authority vested in leader as boss is organizational and hierarchical; the authority vested in leader as messiah is charismatic and interpersonal; and the authority vested in leader as administrator is obligatory, stemming from the obligations that come from serving shared values and purposes. Boss, messiah, and administrator are all roles that you will embrace as school principal.

Figure 4.2   Characteristics of Effective Leaders

Energy and Involvement

1. Physiological
2. Desire to be at the center of the action or "dominant"

Results: high visibility

Competence

1. Intelligence
2. Technical skill
3. Interpersonal skill
    *   Communication
    *   Listening

Personality

1. Sociability
2. Psychological health
3. Charisma

Character

1. Beliefs
2. Security
3. Goals
4. Moral strength

SOURCE: Smith, S. C., and P. K. Piele (2006). *School Leadership Handbook for Excellence,* 4th Ed. Thousand Oaks, CA: Corwin Press.

■ THE NEED FOR CHARISMATIC LEADERS

A charismatic leadership style that catches the attention of students, parents, staff, and the community is imperative in urban schools. Because of these schools' complexity, too frequently apathy, inertia, or chaos reign.

Bass (1990) finds that leaders described as *charismatic* have these personal traits: They are emotionally expressive, self-confident, free from inner conflict, independent, insightful, eloquent, and energetic. They present a clear vision for the future and the conviction that it can be fulfilled.

According to Kouzes and Posner (2002), who conducted discussion sessions using Martin Luther King Jr.'s speech with thousands of business executives, most people find it relatively easy to identify why the speech is so uplifting. It is easy to decipher the code. There is no mystery to its power. The question becomes Can you, an urban school principal, use similar techniques in presentations to a group? Can you become charismatic?

- Can you use images and word pictures?
- Can you use examples that people can relate to?
- Can you talk about traditional values?
- Can you appeal to common beliefs?
- Can you get to know your audience?
- Can you use repetition?
- Can you be positive and hopeful?
- Can you shift from "I" to "we"?
- Can you speak with passion and emotion?
- Can you have personal conviction about the dream?

SOURCE: Adapted from Kouzes and Posner, *The Leadership Challenge* (2002). San Francisco: Jossey-Bass.

Hall (1986) defines a *charismatic leader* as one who values collaboration, democratic decision making, and a commitment to institutionally shared missions and values. Likewise, a charismatic leader possesses desirable individual traits, such as courage, strength of character, and trustworthiness. These traits encourage others to comply with the leader's vision and to participate in the collaborative decision-making process. The leader's inner strength empowers others to act. As Peters (1988) notes, a charismatic leader "exudes mission" (p. 127).

Conger (1989) proposes a theory that identifies the leadership behaviors that influence followers to attribute qualities to a leader. Principals with diverse personalities can duplicate the principles, which are summarized by Sergiovanni (1990b). Followers are more likely to attribute charisma to leaders who achieve the following objectives:

- Advocate a vision that challenges the status quo but still is close enough to be accepted by followers
- Demonstrate convincingly that they are willing to take personal risks, incur high costs, and even make self-sacrifices to achieve their vision
- Pursue a vision and actions that are timely in that they are sensitive to the values, beliefs, and needs of followers on the one hand and to the opportunities inherent in the situation on the other
- Respond to existing dissatisfaction or, if needed, create dissatisfaction in the status quo
- Communicate confidence in themselves and their proposals and enthusiasm about the future prospects for successful implementation of proposals
- Rely on expert power to influence others by demonstrating that they know what they are talking about and can propose solutions that help others to be successful (summarized from Yukl, 1989, pp. 208–209). As this list illustrates, personality alone does not explain charismatic leadership. Followers must be receptive to forming a strong identification with the leader. As stated earlier, this identification may occur for psychological reasons (low self-esteem) or for social reasons (a national state of crisis).

■ URBAN PRINCIPALS' ACADEMY

Charismatic behaviors are critical for the urban school principal. It is imperative that potential school leaders who have demonstrated some of these behaviors are appointed to the principalship. At the district level, an urban principals' academy could be the place that cultivates such behaviors for both experienced and aspiring principals. Such a place would provide mentoring and coaching, internships, and other training and assessment experiences that would strengthen and refine school administrators' skill levels in their quest to become charismatic leaders. If your school district does not have an academy that addresses your charismatic skills, recommend that one be established. Consider the following reasons:

- The reduced influence of social institutions like the church
- The significant negative influence of the media
- The changing nature of the family
- Teachers' and parents' resistance to change even though both demand expedient change (e.g., the urban school is expected to be "all things to all people")
- Drug-related crime and other forms of violence that have spilled over into the schools

Added to these challenges are numerous underfunded state and federal programs. Indeed, the breaking down of barriers requires a person with charisma, vision, a process, and risk taking and entrepreneurial skills.

To meet these and numerous other challenges, a charismatic principal is needed in each urban school. *Do you fit this bill?*

CHARISMA REFLECTIVE PRACTICE EXERCISES

Charisma

Reflective Practice Exercise #1

How do you measure up? Are you aware of the extent to which you possess the necessary knowledge, skills, and attitudes that will make you an effective urban school leader?

Choose one leader each from three of the categories. You do not need to choose a fourth leader.

Figure 4.3   Charismatic Leaders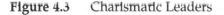

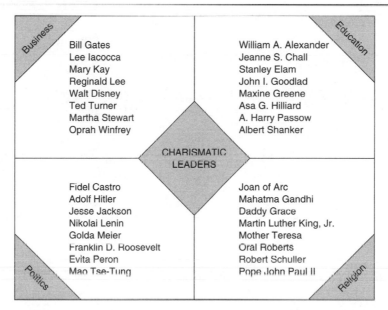

Decide to what extent Smith and Piele's (2006) characteristics of leadership apply to each of your choices.

Leader	Dominant Quality	Rating from 1 to 5
	Energy and Involvement Competence Personality Character	
	Energy and Involvement Competence Personality Character	
	Energy and Involvement Competence Personality Character	

Which characteristic is dominant?

Are all characteristics equally dominant?

What made the leaders charismatic?

Compare/contrast the dominant traits of the three leaders you selected.

Charisma

Reflective Practice Exercise #2

In *Leadership, Empowerment and Management of Change,* Warren Bennis (1994) isolates specific behaviors of charismatic leaders in terms of their ethics.

Unethical Charismatic Leader

- Uses power only for personal gain or impact

- Promotes own personal vision

- Censures critical or opposing views

- Demands own decisions be accepted without question

- One-way communication

- Insensitive to followers' needs

- Relies on convenient external moral standards to satisfy self-interests

Ethical Charismatic Leader

- Uses power to serve others

- Aligns vision with followers' needs and aspirations

- Considers and learns from criticism

- Stimulates followers to think independently and to question the leader's view

- Open, two-way communication

- Coaches, develops, and supports followers; shares recognition with others

- Relies on internal moral standards to satisfy organization and societal interests

1. Although all of the ethical behaviors listed are important, prioritize the list.

2. Which ethical behavior do you think is the hardest for an urban principal to practice? Why?

3. List at least three examples of how you have practiced the following behaviors.
    - Aligns vision with followers' needs and aspirations
    - Stimulates followers to think independently and to question the leader's view
    - Coaches, develops, and supports followers

4. Share your examples with a subordinate or colleague. Is there a match between your self-assessment and your subordinate's or colleague's? Why is this so?

5. Repeat this activity three months from now.

Charisma

Reflective Practice Exercise #3

CHARACTERISTICS OF EFFECTIVE LEADERS

For each statement that follows, decide which of the following answers best applies to you. Place the number of the answer to the left of the statement. Please be honest.

1. Definitely not true   4. Tends to be true

2. Not true   5. True

3. Tends to be not true   6. Especially true

Energy and Involvement

_____ 1. I have a high energy level.

_____ 2. I like being in charge of things, proposing ideas, and initiating action.

_____ 3. I am visible in the school! I walk the hallways, poke my head into classrooms and the cafeteria, visit the in-school suspension room, and participate in activities in classrooms, the media center, the multipurpose room, and assemblies.

_____ 4. I encourage cooperation and collaboration among faculty and staff across disciplines and grade levels.

Competence

_____ 1. I can handle many variables at different degrees of abstraction.

_____ 2. I frequently step back from the immediate situation and use long-term, large-scale patterns and trends.

_____ 3. I apply tacit knowledge. Tacit knowledge includes such things as how to manage myself, how to manage others, and how to manage tasks. (Using simulations, researchers have found that tacit knowledge is a better predictor of performance than intelligence.)

_____ 4. I use my technical knowledge and skill with tact and discretion.

_____ 5. I am able to communicate effectively in face-to-face interactions with a diverse range of individuals and groups.

_____ 6. I can tell a story that resonates with the deepest ideals and aspirations of followers.

_____ 7. I avoid the use of verbal sludge, such as clichés and dry statistics.

_____ 8. I strive to understand situations, read people, and tailor the message accordingly.

_____ 9. I try to accurately reflect the point of view of others after listening to them by restating what was said, applying it, or encouraging feedback.

_____ 10. I try to elicit perceptions, feelings, and concerns of others for problem identification and problem solving.

Personality

_____ 1. I am a personable, friendly person. I am not shy.

_____ 2. I am comfortable working with different kinds of people with various needs, interests, and expectations.

_____ 3. People are at the heart of things, and I desire to work effectively with them.

_____ 4. I am emotionally expressive. I create excitement and enthusiasm about organizational goals.

Character

_____ 1. I believe all students can achieve and achieve at high levels.

_____ 2. I have a mental image of what the school I lead can become.

_____ 3. I believe schools are for learning and students come first.

_____ 4. I am not easily threatened by new ideas or confrontations with others.

_____ 5. I have a high tolerance for ambiguity. I can survive in confusing situations where rules are ill-defined.

_____ 6. I am courageous. To increase student achievement, I am willing to expose myself to circumstances that may generate serious harmful consequences—economic, emotional, or physical.

_____ 7. I can or have articulated clearly several goals to the faculty, staff, and community.

_____ 8. The leader's job is inherently moral: It is not just a matter of doing things right, but of doing the right things. I am a steward. I do the right things.

Arrange the following words under the proper title. Try to match the words. One example has been completed for you.

Words: controlling, flexible, playing it safe, democratic, molding, participating, challenging, forcing, freeing, autocratic, regimenting, enhancing, stifling, releasing, rigid, autocratic, risking

Management	**Leadership**
Managers Do Things Right	Leaders Do the Right Things
Restricting	_Enabling_

Charisma

Reflective Practice Exercise #4

"I HAVE A DREAM" BY DR. MARTIN LUTHER KING, JR.

Dr. King's speech is an example of how a charismatic leader articulates a vision—hopes, dreams, and successes—that inspires people to action. The point of the three previous Exercises is that charisma is *an observable, learnable set of practices that can be mastered.*

1. Search the Internet to locate and listen to Dr. King's "I Have a Dream" speech or simply read the speech aloud to yourself.

2. Imagine yourself at the steps of the Lincoln Memorial and get a feel for how the audience reacted.

3. Organize your observations into two columns, one for what is real and one for what constitutes King's dream.

4. What do you think of this speech? Could you write and deliver such a speech? Is this speech uplifting? If yes, why? If no, why not?

5. Note how you have done the above or how you have seen the above done.

Charisma

Reflective Practice Exercise #5

ALL THINGS TO ALL PEOPLE

Figure 4.4   The Principal

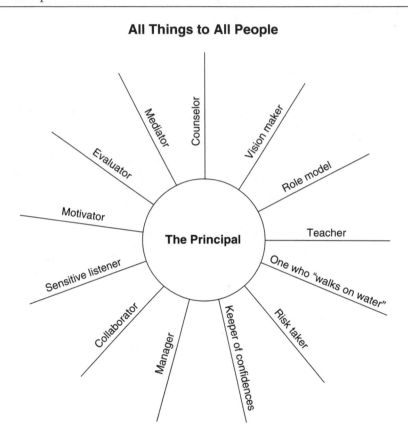

All Things to All People

The Principal

Carefully consider Figure 4.4, which presents a number of roles of the principal.

How does this diagram mirror what you have encountered?

In which of the roles do you feel most comfortable? Why?

In which of the roles do you feel least comfortable? Why?

MY SUNSHINE WHEEL

Use the blank sunshine wheel diagram (Figure 4.5). Put yourself in the middle. For each spoke, write a role you are expected to perform. Include roles from your personal and professional life.

Figure 4.5   Sunshine Wheel

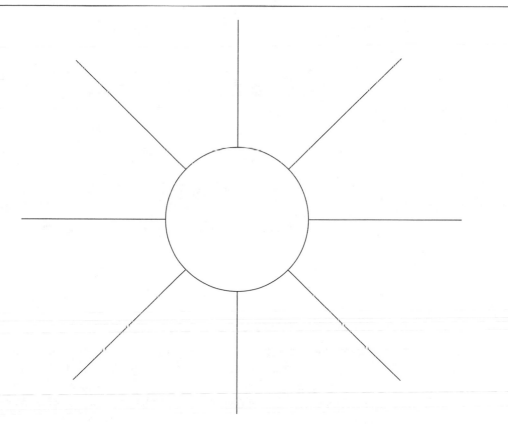

Evaluate your sunshine wheel in terms of those roles that give you the greatest satisfaction and those that give you the least.

List ways in which you can get greater satisfaction from those roles you currently enjoy least.

5

Communication

Sharing Vision and Commitment for Success

School spirit is contagious, and Drew Grammar School had a great case of it. It spread not only throughout the school but throughout the community as well.

At Charles R. Drew Grammar School, the slogan Excellence Has No Boundaries was everywhere. It was printed on the school's stationery and posted prominently throughout the school. Students who had earned the right to wear the bright yellow button proudly displayed it on their clothing every day.

The principal, parents, and community partners also displayed the buttons proudly. Teams had competed to see whose design would be worn. Students cheerfully initiated conversations with teachers and administrators, promoting themselves and others by sharing news about the good deeds that had earned them the button; they also described the accomplishments of their peers and teachers.

The phrase Excellence Has No Boundaries was called out at assemblies; those calling the school or visiting the school were greeted with it. What had begun as a slogan grew to be a call to action and excellence. The students, teachers, and staff internalized the slogan and found that no obstacle was so large as to confound excellence.

THE PRINCIPAL AS COMMUNICATOR   ■

Honest, open communication is an important factor in effecting change (Saphier & King, 1985). Everyone—teachers, staff, students, parents, the school board, partners, and the public at large—evaluates the principal's communication skills all the time. It is common to read letters to local newspaper editors complimenting or criticizing principals' communication skills. Many urban school principals have lost their jobs for failure to communicate effectively with some segment of the community.

According to Lashway (1997), observation, common sense, and intuition help us formulate an image of a good principal, a strong principal, an effective principal. Such principals are often referred to in glowing terms:

- A great communicator
- A people person
- Someone who runs a tight ship
- Someone who keeps the parents at bay
- Someone who knows the district inside and out
- Someone who keeps the building shipshape

Of course, strong leadership is at the heart of each description offered.

Maximizing Human Potential

Honest, open communication is a key to effective leadership performance, organizational credibility, employee trust and motivation, and organizational innovation and productivity (Schwahn & Spady, 1998). Effective leaders are able to involve everyone in pursuing a shared mission; in laymen's terms, they "get the job done through people." Bennis and Nanus (1985) suggest that strong leaders are able to get followers to work "toward goals that represent the values of both the leader and the followers" (p. 85).

The correlation of principals' communication to student achievement, according to Marzano, Waters, and McNulty (2005), is .23. This correlation manifested itself in the researchers' meta-analysis covering a span of 35 years of research. "Communication" is one among 20 research-based skills that are identified as having a correlation to student achievement ranging from .18 to .33. Additional correlations from Marzano et al.'s research that *support the C's* accentuated in this book and their correlation to student achievement follow: .25 Control (defined as order), .25 Curriculum (defined as knowledge of curriculum, instruction, and assessment). .25 Change and/or Courage (defined as change agent), and .18 Caring (defined as relationships) (p. 63).

In her research with 37 highly effective principals and 150 other educators, parents, and school board members, McEwan (2003) includes Communicator and Change Master among the 10 traits of highly effective principals. "Ability to communicate" received the highest number of votes of the 10 traits. Attributes that comprised the trait of Change Master included flexibility, ability to deal with change and ambiguity, ability to convince people to change, and foresight. Caring was listed as an attribute of the trait of Facilitator, garnering 15 votes.

District, state, and national professional associations' assessment tools usually have an oral and written communication component to ensure that principals meet minimum competency in this area. Standard 1 of the Interstate School Leaders Licensure Consortium (ISLLC) Standards for School Leaders addresses principals' ability to communicate to *develop*, to *articulate*, to *implement*, and to *steward*. Both the knowledge and performance indicators for this standard include effective communication.

The importance of the school principal's communication skills has been enunciated by Smith and Andrews (1989). Among the qualities the principal needs are the following:

- The principal as resource provider
- The principal as instructional resource
- The principal as communicator
- The principal as visible presence

Box 5.1 depicts the communication dimensions outlined by Smith and Andrews as those the instructional leader needs.

■ FORMULATING AND PROMOTING A VISION

Arguably the most important thing a principal needs to communicate is a *vision*. Crafting a vision and communicating it to all of the relevant parties, as noted by Smith and Andrews and by Barth, is an essential component of instructional leadership. When formulating a new vision (or mission) statement, or evaluating an existing one, Nanus (1994) suggests using the following criteria:

- Future oriented
- Utopian (leading to better future)
- Appropriate for the organization
- Reflective of high ideals and excellence
- Indicative of the organization's direction
- Capable of inspiring enthusiasm
- Reflective of the organization's uniqueness
- Ambitious

Box 5.2 is an example of a school's vision statement.

For a vision to become a robust presence in your life and the life of your school, it requires careful nurturing. The Communication Reflective Practice Exercises found at the end of this chapter can become critical to your success.

Unlocking the Behaviors That Evidence Effective Communication

Some behaviors that principals practice daily cause teachers to believe the principals are strong communicators and therefore strong leaders. These behaviors include the following (Smith & Andrews, 1989, p. 35):

- Creates improved instructional practice results through interactions between faculty and principal
- Leads formal discussions concerning instruction and student achievement
- Uses clearly communicated criteria for judging staff performance
- Provides a clear vision of what school is all about
- Communicates clearly to the staff regarding instructional matters
- Provides frequent feedback to teachers regarding classroom performance

As you reflect upon the behaviors, how do you fare? Are these routine behaviors you exhibit as you go about performing your duties? Does the principals' evaluation instrument used in your school district assess any of these factors?

Box 5.1   The Principal as Communicator

The instructional leader demonstrates the ability to evaluate and deal effectively with others.

 a. Engages in two-way communication accurately, sensitively, and reliably.
 b. Promotes mutual conflict resolution, problem solving, cooperation, and sharing.
 c. Recognizes what information is appropriate to communicate.

The instructional leader speaks and writes clearly and concisely.

 a. Displays good organizational skills in oral and written communication.
 b. Demonstrates coherence in oral and written communication.
 c. Recognizes needs and interacts appropriately with specific audiences in the educational community.

The instructional leader applies skills and strategies of conflict management that satisfy the interests of both parties in a practical and acceptable manner.

 a. Sees others' viewpoints and clearly articulates them in conflict situations.
 b. Displays the ability to help others arrive at mutually acceptable solutions.
 c. Manages conflict effectively.

The instructional leader facilitates groups in selecting courses of action through problem-solving techniques.

 a. Identifies and collects valid, relevant, and reliable information to accurately assess the current situation.
 b. Develops and analyzes solutions to complex problems.
 c. Develops an implementation plan that includes provisions for evaluation.

The instructional leader demonstrates the ability to use a variety of group process skills in interaction with the staff, parents, and students.

 a. Helps others to develop a commitment to a process for goal achievement.
 b. Assists in formulating the final outcome in a way that can be clearly understood and applied.
 c. Develops and implements procedures for evaluating both process and outcome.

The instructional leader demonstrates skill in working as a team member.

 a. Assesses strengths and weaknesses of team members.
 b. Demonstrates strong group process skills.
 c. Demonstrates the ability to integrate group and personal goals.

SOURCE: W. F. Smith and R. L. Andrews. 1989. *Instructional Leadership: How Principals Make a Difference.* Alexandria, VA: Association for Supervision and Curriculum Development, 17–18. The Association for Supervision and Curriculum Development is a worldwide community of educators advocating sound policies and sharing best practices to achieve the success of each learner. To learn more, visit ASCD at www.ascd.org

Box 5.2   "We Agree" Philosophical Statement

The faculty, staff, students, and communities of our school are devoted to academic excellence and the cultivation of individual strengths and talents in a supportive environment where individual differences and respect for the rights of others guide school and community behavior.

Advisory

We agree that the advisory program is vital to our school if we are to promote the emotional, social, and psychological growth of our students; therefore, teachers will serve as advisors creating a positive atmosphere in which the students will be encouraged to express their concerns.

How Students Learn

We agree that students learn in a variety of ways; therefore, we shall provide in our classrooms (a) problem-solving opportunities that encourage deductive/inductive reasoning, (b) the lecture method followed by guided practice and small group instruction, (c) opportunities for discovery through interest-centered activities and peer tutoring, (d) lessons that promote multisensory perception, and (e) many meaningful, realistic sharing experiences.

School and Community

We agree that the school and community should cooperate with each other for the common good of both agencies; therefore, we shall (a) encourage civic pride in our students through participation in community projects and activities, and ask the community to support school activities; and (b) use community resources and persons in the classroom where feasible.

School Organization

We agree that as a middle school we must promote the multidisciplinary and team teaching approaches to education; therefore, we will be organized by grade level into several small units of teams with teachers from various departments, special subject area teachers, counselors, and support staff working together with the assigned administrators to help students reach their maximum potential.

Curriculum

We agree that our curriculum as prescribed by Baltimore Public Schools should form a framework from which can be developed a flexible program of instruction for middle school students; therefore, as we approach our teaming efforts we will strive to promote common goals, keeping in mind the required components of local and state curriculum mandates.

Remember, formal and informal meetings, MBWA encounters, newsletters, policy documents, and posted opportunities for teachers to enhance their professional development provide opportunities for you to promote the shared vision.

COLLEGIALITY CONVERSATIONS   ■

In *Improving Schools From Within,* Barth (1990) suggests that the conversations that schools need to have should be based upon the norm of *collegiality.* Collegiality conversations focus upon what is occurring in the school and, in particular, upon what needs to be done to improve the quality of education for students. Barth recognizes that such conversations may, by their very nature, cause the people who work in a school to come into conflict with one another on occasion; however, he also believes that until educators move beyond the need to get along and begin to act as professionals, they will continue doing themselves and their students a grave disservice.

COMMUNICATING WITH   ■
STUDENTS AND PARENTS

How do you communicate to students the value of their opinions in the operation of the school? Are multiple opportunities for exchanging information and ideas with students available in your school? Are students told concretely, in a variety of ways, that they are expected to speak up and evaluate existing communication options? Communication Reflective Practice Exercises enumerate beginning and ongoing communication strategies to use with students.

Elementary and middle school principals will need to increase the number of opportunities that students have to review the school's student handbook. To do so is developmentally responsive. Younger students need more frequent reviews of policies and practices. These students' parents will become argumentative when their children are disciplined if an entire marking period has expired since the school last reviewed the rules with their children.

Communicating With Parents

Throughout the surveys for students on control, caring, and communication, there are items that speak to parent participation. Numerous publications and Web sites exist to strengthen schools' outreach to parents and families. It is well known that when families, educators, and communities all work together, schools get better and students get the high-quality education they need (Decker et al., 1994).

Although the purpose is not to review existing literature on parent involvement—barriers, benefits, effective strategies, evaluation tools—it would be remiss not to (1) underscore the importance of a well-thought-out plan, (2) share seven principles for developing a family-school partnership,

(3) outline six widely used practices of school-family-community partnerships, and (4) provide three family-friendly tools for your use.

Effective communication starts with a well-thought-out plan, and a good plan of communication starts with the school principal (Northwest Regional Educational Laboratory, n.d.). A well-designed communication plan can result in parents improving their parenting skills. Various models exist for the components of a plan. There is no blueprint for urban schools to communicate and collaborate effectively with families. Because schools are different, there is no single model, no one set of practices or characteristics to which one can point and say, "Aha! This is the definitive model." But all schools that work well with families share a fundamental set of seven principles (see Box 5.3).

Parents of urban school students are diverse, multicultural, highly educated, and sometimes uneducated. It is not uncommon for adults who are known as "Auntie" or "Uncle," with no biological relationship, to report to a parent conference on behalf of a student. Some parents do not speak English. Others are teenagers, middle aged, or they may be grandparents. Some parents are homeless. Since a significant number of urban students are wards of the state, some "parents" are juvenile justice probation officers, social workers, group home directors, or foster parents. This spectrum of adults appearing in the school office on behalf of urban students is vast. These adults' communication skills vary as well.

Frequently, in urban schools parents will walk into the office and demand to see the principal. If the principal is not available, an emotional outburst may ensue. A demand might be made to readmit the student immediately because the parent cannot take another day off from work to be "bothered with the mess where school administrators have not been fair." There is usually a threat to report the school staff's unfairness, insensitivity, and bias against the child to the district superintendent and/or the principal's supervisor. It is not uncommon for two students and their parents to report to the school for a mediation conference and for an outburst to occur before the administrator can escort the two factions into a conference area. What is the urban school principal to do?

Adherence to the following strategy or one similar should reduce the number of parent outbursts occurring in public areas in your school.

1. Whether the parent has an appointment or not, office staff should greet the person with a smile, get the person to sign in, and if a conference room is available, lead the person to the area. Offer the person something to drink, preferably water. (Angry parents have been known to throw hot coffee or tea on school staff in the heat of the moment, so a hot drink should not be offered.)

2. Staff should inform the parent(s) that someone will be with him or her shortly. (The important point here is that the angry parent has been moved out of the public area.) If someone other than the principal will be meeting with the parent, the parent should be told this.

3. If the parent refuses to be respectful, school security or another appropriate staff member should be contacted for assistance. The school security officer should remain for the duration of the conference, if possible.

4. The conference should commence with the principal welcoming the parents with a smile.

   a. The parent should be thanked for coming.

   b. The principal should outline the behavior expectation during the conference. The parent should be told that the conference will be terminated if the ground rules are not followed.

5. Allow the parent and child to share their perspectives of what happened before questions are asked.

6. Once the parents and child are finished with their presentations, the principal should ask clarifying questions, summarize critical points, and end with asking the parent, "What do you think should be done to solve this problem?"

7. It is recommended that the principal strike a happy medium by including a portion of what the parent thinks is equitable in the solution (if what is wanted is legal and fair and is within the limits of the principal's authority and school district policy and procedures). This way, the principal increases his or her chances of keeping the lines of communications open with this parent, who is sure to return to the school office at a future date because of his child's behavior.

Alternate sites for the parent meeting could be the parent resource center, the guidance counselor's office, the grade-level administrator's office, or the concerned teacher's classroom if the teacher is not teaching at the time of the visit.

Box 5.3   Seven Principles for Working Well With Families

Principle 1: Every aspect of the school climate is open, helpful, and friendly.

Principle 2: Communications with families (whether about school policies and programs or about their own children) are frequent, clear, and two-way.

Principle 3: Families are treated as collaborators in the educational process with a strong complementary role to play in their children's schooling and learning behavior.

Principle 4: Families are encouraged, both formally and informally, to comment on school policies and (on some issues) to share in the decision-making process.

Principle 5: The school recognizes its responsibility to forge a partnership with all families in the school, not simply those most easily available. This includes parents who work outside the home, divorced parents without custody, and families of minority race and language.

Principle 6: The principal and other school administrators actively express and promote the philosophy of partnership with all families.

Principle 7: The school encourages volunteer participation by families and the community at large.

SOURCE: L. E. Decker et al. 1994. *Home-School-Community Relations.* Charlottesville, VA: Mid-Atlantic Center for Community Education, University of Virginia.

Six Types of Involvement

The seven principles enumerated in Box 5.3 complement Epstein's six types of involvement (Epstein, Sanders, Simon, Clark Salinas, Rodriguez Jansorn, & Van Voorhis, 1997). Epstein et al.'s types are codified in an inventory, creating a comprehensive program of school, family, and community partnerships. Box 5.4 lists the six types and the roles of schools.

Box 5.4   Epstein's Six Types of Involvement

Type 1. Parenting: Basic responsibilities of families. Schools should assist families with parenting skills, with managing home conditions to support children as students, and assist educators in understanding families.

Type 2. Communicating: Basic responsibilities of schools. Schools design effective forms of communication with each parent (about school programs and children's progress).

Type 3. Volunteering: Involvement at and for the school. Schools recruit and organize parent help and support.

Type 4. Learning at Home: Involvement in academic activities. Schools give parents ideas on how to help their children at home.

Type 5. Decision Making: Participation and leadership. Schools include families as participants in school decisions and develop parent leaders and representatives.

Type 6. Collaboration With the Community: Schools, families, and students must establish connections with agencies, businesses, cultural groups, and community organizations.

SOURCE: Adapted from Epstein, J., et al., 2002. *School, Family, and Community Partnerships: Your Handbook for Action.* Thousand Oaks, CA: Corwin Press.

Taking Stock

A similar report card contains 20 indicators and a different kind of grading protocol. The National Committee for Citizens in Education developed this protocol in 1993. Taking Stock (Form 5.2) is a systematic way to look at the school's relationship with families from a number of perspectives. It is a tool for self-evaluation to identify strengths and weaknesses. Finally, it is a practical approach to improving student achievement by increasing parent involvement (and thereby increasing the quantity and quality of your communications with parents).

Share the survey with the appropriate committee in your school. Have the committee develop a plan for its use. Implement the plan and use the results as part of your school's action plan for school improvement. Implement specific activities this school year. Do not delay until the next academic school year.

Unlocking the Elements of a Parent-Friendly School

How family-friendly is your school? What grade would you give your school for its family friendliness—A? B? Some other grade? What criteria did you use to decide the grade you gave your school? Is your school father friendly?

(Continued)

The United States Department of Education Office of Educational Research and Improvement published a comprehensive booklet, *Reaching All Families, Creating Family-Friendly Schools* (Moles, 1996), to stimulate thinking and discussion about how schools can better involve all families, regardless of family circumstances or student performance. The booklet is available by calling 800-USA-LEARN. The user-friendly booklet contains 18 strategies in five categories.

Nontraditional Families

To close out this section on communicating with families, think about nontraditional families in your outreach activities. For example, more and more grandparents, blended families, and fathers are raising their children. It is not unusual in urban schools for a minority male—father, uncle, grandfather, mother's former boyfriend—to be the sole adult responsible for children in attendance at your school. Many of us assume fathers don't want to be involved, yet research shows they do, according to the authors of *Getting Men Involved: Strategies for Early Childhood Programs* (Levine, Murphy, & Wilson, 1993). You and your staff have to create a father-friendly environment, one that beckons men and empowers them to help children. Form 5.3, a father-friendly checklist, is provided as a foundation tool for this purpose.

(Continued)

How do you know? Do you and your staff use specifically designed communication strategies to involve fathers in your school?

To put your school's family friendliness to the test, reproduce the Report Card for All Visitors (Form 5.1) and ask every visitor who enters the building to complete it. At the end of two weeks, examine the responses and share them with the faculty and staff. You might want to administer the survey and summarize, disseminate, and discuss it at least three times a year.

Unlocking the Ability to Communicate Excellence

Carefully consider the scenario that opened this chapter. What role, if any, does a slogan play in fostering school spirit and esprit de corps at your school? Think of ways that you could use a slogan to help address a challenge at your school.

As you step up your efforts to involve men, the authors of *Getting Men Involved* caution, "don't slight women." Let them know you are making special efforts. Make sure programs and opportunities are offered to men and women equitably. Don't allow men to automatically assume positions of power, like PTA president or committee chairperson.

COMMUNICATING WITH PARTNERS ■

Frequently, schools are expected to resolve society's social and economic ills; when the schools' attempted reforms fail to produce quick fixes, critics make a scapegoat of their visible leadership. Schools do not exist in a vacuum, and none can succeed without community support that includes parents, organizations, institutions, agencies, and various groups. The wise school principal uses this fact to augment the limited resources at hand to address the multiple challenges his or her school faces.

Two major school reports, *Breaking Ranks* (NASSP, 1996) and *Turning Points* (Carnegie Council on Adolescent Development, 1989), recommend

Form 5.1

Report Card for All Visitors

Name of Your School: _____

Introduction: This report card is designed to improve communication and understanding between families and school staff. Please complete it and leave it with us, or take it home and return it to school with your child or by mail. Thank you.

Key: Please respond to the items by using a letter from this key.

A = Excellent B = Good C = Fair D = Poor F = Fail I = Incomplete information or can't decide

ITEMS

_____ 1. How do you rate the appearance and upkeep of our school and classrooms?

_____ 2. How do you rate your child's academic progress at our school?

_____ 3. How do you rate our school's communication with the home (telephone contact, grade reports, notes, newsletters)?

_____ 4. How do you rate discipline at our school?

_____ 5. How do you rate your child's attitude toward this school?

---

that schools establish and sustain partnerships with parents, public officials, community agencies, colleges and universities, business representatives, neighboring schools, and others. A partnership approach provides a method for involving many segments of a community in addressing multiple school needs.

Partnerships are expected and are usually included as one criterion on the principal's evaluation form. As an urban school principal, you must use communication strategies that address the diverse opinions the public has of your school.

Communication, Communication, Communication

Communication is one of many key behaviors you must use to carry out the responsibility with which you are charged. "Failure to communicate" is frequently the stated reason for urban schools losing well-funded and well-staffed business partners. Partners' expectations and benefits should be clear to everyone involved. This is essential to promote understanding and increase the level of trust. One question that should focus your midyear and year-end evaluations is "Will we be able to measure the difference these people make in our program, or are we really involved in a public relations program?" You should evaluate all services and interaction resulting from the partnership. For steps to build the partnerships, consult school partnerships manuals published by the principals'

Form 5.2

Taking Stock: A Report Card

Directions: Grade each of the following on a scale of 1–4, with 4 being excellent. Calculate the average for each category.

	Grade	Final Grade
Reaching Out to Families		
1. Communicating often and openly with families	_____	
2. Reaching all cultural and language groups	_____	
3. Reaching working and single parents	_____	
4. Extra efforts to reach all families	_____	
		_____
Welcoming Families to the School Building		
5. School's welcome to families	_____	
6. Open and available school and staff	_____	
7. Encouraging volunteers	_____	
8. Active PTA/PTO activities	_____	
9. Major PTA/PTO activities	_____	
10. Reaching out to the community	_____	
		_____
Developing Strong Relationships		
11. Teachers communicate with parents	_____	
12. Parent-teacher partnership	_____	
13. Parent-principal partnership	_____	
14. Parents involved in decision making	_____	
15. School-parent involvement policy exists	_____	
		_____
Helping Parents Understand the Curriculum		
16. Information about the curriculum	_____	
17. Goals for student achievement	_____	
18. Information on student performance	_____	
		_____
Helping Parents Be More Effective		
19. School supports parents	_____	
20. School connects to community services	_____	
		_____

A. 3.2–4.0   Great job. Keep up the excellent work!

B. 2.6–3.1   Good work. A little more will put you on top!

C. 2.0–2.5   Solid beginning. Time for some next steps!

U. 1.0–1.9   Needs improvement. Let's get to work!

Form 5.3

Is Your School Father-Friendly?

Here is a checklist to help you assess just how friendly your school is to fathers. If your school isn't doing these things, or isn't doing them well, now's a good time to start planning improvements.

_____   1.   Actively and continuously encourage all men to participate—regardless of their backgrounds, attitude, limitations, or age.

_____   2.   Send a copy of notices to fathers not living in the home.

_____   3.   Tell men directly (not through mothers) that the school needs their involvement.

_____   4.   Display photos or drawings and publish stories of men involved with children at school.

_____   5.   Show a genuine interest in fathers by greeting them at the door and asking them casual questions, like "So what have you been up to lately?"

_____   6.   Give both Dads and Moms specific activities to do with their children at home, and ask them to do specific "jobs" at school.

_____   7.   Find out what men are interested in, what they would like to do, and what information/help/skills they need.

_____   8.   Provide programs and activities geared to meet the specific needs of fathers and other significant male adults in students' lives.

_____   9.   Schedule home visits, conferences, and other events at a time when fathers can attend.

_____   10.   Call or visit men when they don't attend a planned event, and ask them why.

_____   11.   Speak to mothers and fathers equally when they are both present at meetings, conferences, or home visits.

_____   12.   Offer something that is unique for men only, like a "Fathers' Club" or weekly "Donuts for Dads" coffees.

_____   13.   Include in the parent room *Sports Illustrated,* special books and notices for Dads, and other items of interest to men.

_____   14.   Use men to recruit fathers and other male volunteers in the community.

_____   15.   Recognize Dads' contributions as well as Moms'.

---

associations (NAESP and NASSP). Regular meetings with school partners will ensure that lines of communication are open and that the school addresses problems in a timely manner.

Key Communicators

The strategy called Key Communicators will allow you to keep your school's shared vision prominent in the minds of your supporters.

Key communicators are supportive people—internal and external—who are kept well informed about your school. Their job is twofold:

- To quickly spread accurate and supportive information to other members of the community
- To be listening posts in the school and community, alerting the school principal to rumors and concerns

Almost anyone can be a key communicator, but the people selected should represent a cross-section of the community and have two traits:

- Be respected and listened to in his or her circle of contacts, regardless of the size of the circle
- Be supportive of the school and its successful operation, especially during times of stress

Seven tips will help you establish and maintain good communication with your key communicators:

1. Identify people who share opinions with others about your school. They might be businesspeople, volunteers, bus drivers, crossing guards, substitutes, parents, former students, or former students' parents.

2. Call each person and invite him or her to become a key communicator. Invite them all to come to one meeting, stressing that there will not be additional meetings. *Explain your school's shared vision.* Briefly explain the key communicator concept. Assure them that you are aware of their interest in the school and that you would like them to be key communicators to receive and share information—to be two-way communicators.

3. Distribute envelopes containing informational items. Contents could consist of the school mission/vision statement, a school newsletter, a pertinent staff bulletin or two, and a calendar with schedules (including testing schedule, if possible).

4. Ask these key communicators to call you. Explain your need to know if something is occurring that affects the students or school, or if something has been said that sounds like a rumor. Promise that you, in turn, will keep them informed.

5. Keep a supply of envelopes addressed to your key communicators, or make a list of them on your computer. If an incident warrants, a simple e-mail or letter of explanation to these people before the story reaches the newspapers or is exaggerated by the rumor mill will pay great dividends in credibility. Also, set up a telephone chain for quicker response if the need arises.

6. Be ready for one or more of the following to occur: Additional people will call and ask to be one of your key communicators; the credibility of your school information will increase; an information call from a key communicator will provide a key to solving a problem. Your *vision* will become well known in the community.

7. At the end of the year, invite the key communicators to school. Thank them for their support. Consider giving them a certificate, a small gift, or an admission ticket to a school event (Decker et al., 1994).

**Unlocking Implementation
of an Important Strategy**

Think about the Key Communicators strategy. List three reasons why you cannot implement the strategy. List three benefits of implementing the strategy.

Share the strategy with your administrative team. Ask them to list three reasons why it would not be a good idea to implement the strategy at this time. Ask them to list three benefits of implementing the strategy.

Compare lists. What are the similarities? The differences? Decide as a team whether or not to implement the strategy.

Public Relations

Public relations refers to the school's deliberate efforts to influence community opinion and win community support. Media relations are not easy, and most urban school districts have a public relations office to build understanding about the school district. This office's efforts are usually insufficient because neighborhood schools bear the brunt of negative media coverage concerning incidents occurring in and around schools. More often than not, you find yourself spending 10% to 15% of your time on public relations tasks.

■ SIX COMMUNICATION TRAPS

The effective communicator avoids traps that the not-so-effective communicator continually falls into. Here are six of those traps with some tips on how to avoid them. These tips are summarized in *Communication Briefings* by Lin Grensing-Pophal (1996).

1. Using Only One Medium

To make sure your message gets through, you have many communication options: phone, in person, fax, e-mail, memo, meetings. The method you choose depends on your audience. Don't force your communication style on others.

2. Demanding, Not Requesting

A request is always more readily accepted than a demand. And that's even more the case when your request gives a reason that includes a benefit for those who comply with your request.

3. Personalizing Criticism

Focus on objective behaviors, not on judgments. And don't criticize someone's character or abilities. You are more likely to be heard if you can show how what you're asking meets the organization's needs or needs shared by you and the person with whom you are communicating.

4. "Forgetting" to Listen

Listening skills are the most critical part of any interpersonal communication, but we often fail at this step because of a preoccupation with our own internal conversations. The first step to better listening skills is to develop patience. The next step is to understand that listening is not a one-way process; effective communication requires a two-way exchange of information. To truly communicate, we must "send back" what we've listened to in an effort to verify our perceptions. This results in the necessary two-way exchange and leads to effective communication.

5. Reacting Defensively

The best defense against defensiveness is to keep your mental monitor attuned to your reactions. Take a deep breath and redouble your efforts to focus on the communication. Walk away if you have to, but be sure to indicate that you intend to resume the exchange and say when.

6. Communicating an "Entitlement" Attitude

Poor communicators act as though everyone else owes them respect and cooperation. They do not seem to grasp this simple communication fact: You should never fail to offer thanks, encouragement, and positive feedback to the people you deal with. They'll appreciate it, and it will build your reputation as an effective and fair communicator.

SOURCE: From Grensing-Pophal, L. 1996. Seven "Communication Traps and How You Can Avoid Them," *Communication Briefings.* 15(6): 8a–8ab. Alexandria, VA: Briefings Publishing Group.

Unlocking the Public Relations Challenge

The following eight rules will aid you with the unending responsibility of communicating with the public.

1. Be a square shooter (accuracy-integrity-performance). Don't favor one news outlet over another.

2. Give service. Provide interesting, timely stories and pictures in a form and at a time in which the press can use them.

3. Don't beg or carp. Advertising belongs in the advertising department. Know the difference between advertising and news—newspeople do.

4. Don't ask to have a story killed. The way to keep unfavorable stories out of the press is to prevent situations that produce such stories. Bad news never improves with age.

5. Avoid talking "off the record." If you don't want a statement quoted, don't make it.

6. Don't flood the media with your "news."

7. Keep your lists up to date.

8. Remember that a good press relationship must be earned.

COMMUNICATION REFLECTIVE PRACTICE EXERCISES

Communication

Reflective Practice Exercise #1

LISTENING TO THE STUDENT VOICE

It is important that students know that their opinions are valued. When you show that you value students' input, you personalize the school and empower students to be active problem solvers. By implementing the following ideas, you may be better able to hear your students' voices.

1. Review the activities with three different focus groups of students. Ask each group to add to the list.

2. Ask students to help develop and/or revise strategies and procedures for the following:

   - Reviewing the student handbook with students who do not register at the beginning of the school year
   - Reviewing the school's orientation program for new students
   - Requesting a conference with the counselor and the school principal
   - Displaying existing school rules prominently throughout the school
   - Establishing classroom rules regarding things such as homework and class participation
   - Determining membership on the school newspaper (e.g., how to increase the number of students involved with its development and publication)
   - Determining membership in the student council
   - Deciding the availability of student clubs
   - Deciding any other student-centered practice you like

3. In two weeks, report to the students which of their ideas you will present to the faculty for adoption and implementation.

Communication

Reflective Practice Exercise #2

INITIATING COMMUNICATION WITH STUDENTS

Determine whether or not the statements that follow accurately reflect your school's communication practices. For those statements you find do not reflect what your school is doing, undertake an action plan in concert with your governing team to promote more meaningful communication between all partners.

Goal: To provide opportunities for the exchange of information and ideas for the purpose of improving dialogue among the various school sectors.

	Yes	No
Students review the handbook in classroom settings at least twice yearly. There is a process whereby new registrants review the student handbook.	☐	☐
The school regularly communicates expectations of academic achievement via the public address system, in student publications, and in materials sent home to parents.	☐	☐
An orientation program exists for each level of students (e.g., 6th/9th grade). This program clearly outlines expectations and ways students can access school resources.	☐	☐
Students have an anonymous way to report the existence of weapons or drugs on school premises.	☐	☐
The procedure for students to request a conference with a counselor or any other adult is widely publicized.	☐	☐
Administrators are visible during each lunch period.	☐	☐
Student suggestion boxes are located in neutral places (e.g., library, cafeteria, study hall) in the school. Action taken on students' suggestions is published in student publications and/or announced on the public address system.	☐	☐
Teachers are required to send home course syllabi, an outline of their class objectives, and information on homework expectations, how they may be contacted, and how parents may help.	☐	☐
Parents are provided with information about their child's progress, including results on standardized tests, in a timely manner.	☐	☐

Communication

Reflective Practice Exercise #3

STABILIZING COMMUNICATION WITH STUDENTS

Determine whether or not the statements that follow accurately reflect your school's communication practices. For those statements you find do not reflect what your school is doing, undertake an action plan in concert with your governing team to promote more meaningful communication between all partners.

Goal: To nurture student excellence in the process of supporting their initiatives and soliciting their input in decision making and school governance.

	Yes	No
Workshops on such topics as college admission and financial aid for college are conducted at least three times a year.	☐	☐
The student newspaper and other publications (literary magazine) are entered into contests and competitions. The student body is informed about this.	☐	☐
Individual students' outstanding achievement and the school's recognition of excellence are communicated to students through the student newspaper, other student publications, community papers, and other media.	☐	☐
The principal meets with the student council leadership group monthly.	☐	☐
The principal meets with an umbrella group of student leaders monthly.	☐	☐
Parent-teacher-student report card conferences are held each marking period.	☐	☐
Students participate in the planning and delivery of all schoolwide assemblies.	☐	☐
Administrators make appearances at all student activity functions (e.g., plays, induction ceremonies for academic achievers, musical concerts). Appearances are not limited to athletic events.	☐	☐
Administrators visit classrooms daily and compliment, as appropriate, teachers and students for their achievements.	☐	☐
The principal has a column in the student newspaper.	☐	☐

Communication

Reflective Practice Exercise #4

SUSTAINING EFFECTIVE COMMUNICATION
WITH STUDENTS

Determine whether or not the statements that follow accurately reflect your school's communication practices. For those statements you find do not reflect what your school is doing, undertake an action plan in concert with your governing team to promote more meaningful communication between all partners.

Goal: To ensure students' voice in school decision making and school governance.

	Yes	No
Student focus groups are convened to assess school climate.	☐	☐
Biannually a student climate survey is administered.	☐	☐
Special evening meetings are held for students "at risk" academically. (They are held in the evenings to accommodate working parents.)	☐	☐
Press releases about individual students' achievements are disseminated to community papers and other media on a regular basis.	☐	☐
Students are provided opportunities to engage in cross-cultural communications.	☐	☐

Communication

Reflective Practice Exercise #5

COMMUNICATING WITH FACULTY AND STAFF

For each of the communication strategies listed on the left below, check one column: *Quick Fixes* (those ideas that are important and can be accomplished quickly by you or independently by others), *Out of Our Hands* (ideas that are not realistic given the present circumstances), or *Definite Possibilities* (the rest of the ideas).

Quick Fixes, Out of Our Hands, Definite Possibilities

Communication Strategy	*Quick Fixes*	*Out of Our Hands*	*Definite Possibilities*
Share and exchange information with faculty and staff to enhance the educational environment for students and to promote the efficient operation of the school.			
Faculty/department/team meetings are held on a regular basis. The overarching purpose of such meetings is to ensure that teachers understand their role in the achievement of the school district's instructional goals, the school's goals, and their respective departmental goals.			
Teachers are encouraged to suggest improvements in operational procedures (at meetings, through a suggestion box, in departments, in the instructional council, etc.).			
Meetings are held for the specific purpose of discussing achievement tests and other performance data.			
The faculty is involved in the design of academic programs.			
Faculty/staff input is encouraged to develop programs that recognize their outstanding achievements (e.g., attendance, instruction, programming, assistance for the effectiveness of the total school program).			

Communication Strategy	Quick Fixes	Out of Our Hands	Definite Possibilities
Several bulletin boards exist in the school where information about professional enhancement opportunities is posted.			
A daily/weekly bulletin is disseminated to all staff.			
School administrators are visible, making a complete walk around the building (inside) at least twice daily.			
A clear policy exists that stipulates that school administrators may visit classrooms informally to observe and collect data.			

Concentrate future team efforts on the "Definite Possibilities" list. Eliminate the "Out of Our Hands" list, but don't ignore the ideas in the "Quick Fixes" list, for they may be the source of early and easy successes. You or individual volunteers may tackle those issues, freeing the group to address more complex ideas.

Communication

Reflective Practice Exercise #6

STABILIZING COMMUNICATION WITH ADULTS

Determine whether or not the statements that follow accurately reflect your school's communication practices. For those statements you find do not reflect what your school is doing, undertake an action plan in concert with your governing team to promote more meaningful communication between all partners.

Goal: To share and exchange information with faculty and staff to enhance the educational environment for students and to promote the efficient operation of the school.

	Yes	No
Periodic meetings are convened to discuss current trends, issues, and concerns in education. Reading materials are procured and housed in the professional library for this purpose.	☐	☐
Funds from the school's budget (and/or budgets funded by grants or business partners) are used to pay for faculty and staff's attendance at professional development conferences/workshops/seminars.	☐	☐
Faculty and staff attending professional conferences funded by the school are required to share what they learn and to implement at least two ideas gleaned. A system exists to monitor this requirement.	☐	☐
Semester/yearly reports are generated to summarize faculty and staff's	☐	☐

    __ attendance at conferences/workshops/seminars

    __ ideas adopted as a result of a suggestion made

    __ departments' efforts to achieve system and school goals

    __ departments' participation in contests, competitions, etc.

    __ special programs initiated, etc.

Faculty and staff may make appointments to see the principal and do so within three days of the request, barring an emergency.	☐	☐

6

Curriculum

The Tool for Instructional Leadership

It's Dr. Diaz's first staff meeting of a new school year at a school to which she is newly assigned. Right off the bat there's contentiousness.

"The scope and sequence is a mile wide and an inch deep," a voice offers from the back of the room.

Before Dr. Diaz can answer, another voice rings out. "We only have 180 instructional days to teach to a standards document that is bigger than a Manhattan phone book," a veteran teacher complains.

Dr. Diaz has already reviewed the teachers' lesson plans for the first week. The first, second, and third grades each begin with a unit on Native American peoples. The third grade spends 10 of the instructional days taking state-mandated tests.

"If you think we're not going on our overnight lock-in at the planetarium just because the solar system is now assigned to the sixth grade, you've got another think coming," a fifth-grade teacher offers in a less than collegial tone.

"What a mandate!" the principal says under her breath. No one ever said being an urban school principal was going to be easy.

■ ATTAINING STUDENT ACHIEVEMENT THROUGH INSTRUCTIONAL LEADERSHIP

Unlocking Consensus Through Instructional Leadership

Take a look at the scenario that opens this chapter. Have you ever attended a staff meeting that sounded anything like it? Reflect on your experience with standards and curriculum documents. Do you think that a mandated standards-based curriculum is the key to student achievement? What can be done to get your staff to buy into the merit of a particular curricular initiative?

Curriculum leadership is the very essence of instructional leadership. Moreover, curriculum work is constant. At times other specific school improvement goals must take priority over curriculum articulation. Yet curriculum articulation is vital to the core outcomes of school improvement, and the quality of the curriculum is critically linked to student achievement. Therefore, curriculum work must be perceived as a continuous process.

■ PROFESSIONAL AND PERSONAL READINESS

Effective school principals practice lifelong learning behaviors. The principalship demands this. Although no one expects you to become an expert in each area for which you have responsibility, you must be conversant with pertinent information that will allow you to facilitate and lead for systemic reform as needed. For instruction and curriculum initiatives, you need to be able to engage your staff and others in intelligent conversations about the following:

- The changing nature of society and your community
- The changing nature of students
- New developments in technology
- Current research on teaching, learning, and curriculum

As a leader who will use curriculum as a tool for instructional leadership, you need to be knowledgeable about the following:

- Major national developments in the general area of curriculum
- General curriculum trends in each subject area
- Significant features of new curricula to be implemented
- Methods for observing the effective implementation of curricula (Glatthorn, 1994)

Information Resources

The principals' national associations, the U.S. Department of Education's 10 regional educational laboratories, the various subject area associations, and the National Governors' Association are resources for getting information you need.

PROFESSIONAL ASSOCIATIONS TARGET ■ CURRICULUM LEADERSHIP

The National Association of Elementary School Principals' (NAESP) *Standards for Quality Elementary and Middle Schools* (1996) includes a Curriculum and Instruction Standard that principals are expected to address and families and communities are expected to evaluate. Specifically, the association states, "In a quality school, the principal guides the instructional program toward the achievement of clearly defined curricular goals and objectives" (p. 11). The principal's role is further clarified by underscoring school climate issues that contribute to teachers' risk taking for curricular implementation and doing what is best for students. At the same time, the principal is expected to "monitor the school's curriculum, instruction, and assessment procedures" (p. 12).

In *Breaking Ranks* (NASSP, 1996), the National Association of Secondary School Principals proposes nine strategies that principals must use so that the high school curriculum can offer both substance and practicality to prepare students for the nine purposes of high school. (The purposes are outlined in Box 6.1.) The strategies focus on the following objectives:

- A set of essential learnings
- Curricular integration
- Teachers' behaviors in the design process
- Curriculum content
- Assessment and the use of a Personal Plan for Progress to meet individual student needs
- Cocurricular activities as extensions of academic learning
- Curriculum articulation with elementary and middle schools

It is clear then, according to the principals' association, that your attention to curriculum is central to your role as principal.

Box 6.1 Nine Purposes of High School

1. High school is, above all else, a learning community and each school must commit itself to expecting demonstrated academic achievement for every student in accord with standards that can stand up to national scrutiny.

2. High school must function as a transitional experience, getting each student ready for the next stage of life, whatever it may be for that individual, with the understanding that, ultimately, each person needs to earn a living.

3. High school must be a gateway to multiple options.

4. High school must prepare each student to be a lifelong learner.

5. High school must provide an underpinning for good citizenship and for full participation in the life of a democracy.

(Continued)

Box 6.1 (Continued)

6. High school must play a role in the personal development of young people as social beings who have needs beyond those that are strictly academic.

7. High school must lay a foundation for students to be able to participate comfortably in an increasingly technological society.

8. High school must equip young people for life in a country and a world in which interdependency will link their destiny to that of others, however different those others may be from them.

9. High school must be an institution that unabashedly advocates in behalf of young people.

SOURCE: *Breaking Ranks: Changing an American Institution. Copyright (1996) National Association of Secondary School Principals. www.principals.org. Reprinted with permission.*

■ CURRICULUM LEADERSHIP RESEARCH

Principals desiring to improve their schools cannot be content merely to coordinate responses and activities of individual teachers. Instead, they must strive to create staff synergy by visualizing and designing workable models of curricular unity.

English (2000) sees curricular as comprising three interactive parts:

- The written curriculum
- The taught curriculum
- The tested curriculum

These elements may exist in school but often function independently of one another. Course content can bear little relationship to tests or to curriculum guide statements. In such cases, trying to use measurement data or tests to improve teaching is futile.

According to English (1987), one step principals can take to implement curricular unity is to dismantle ambiguous curriculum statements and substitute "valid and concise statements of work content" (p. 36). They must also be prepared to acquire valid assessment tools, ensure congruency of textbooks with curriculum and tests, monitor curriculum delivery, and obtain adequate feedback as a decision-making guideline.

Two research studies that focus specifically on urban school principals' attention to curriculum and instructional leadership are discussed below. As you read the descriptions, think about how the research questions asked would play out in your school district.

Polite, McClure, and Rollie (1997) report on the process and outcome of shadowing encounters with 16 urban middle school principals. The professional development curriculum that guided the principals toward becoming student-centered had five elements. Here, only one element is discussed—Leader in Promoting Students' Cognitive Development. Upon completion of the shadowing encounter and an in-depth follow-up interview, each principal was asked two questions:

1. What do I tend to do with my time daily?

2. What do my collective work behaviors mean with respect to instructional leadership for my school?

Using Glasman's typology of six principal roles and the measures of principal leadership behavior, Blank (1987) studied 32 urban comprehensive high schools to determine the extent to which urban high school principals provided leadership and in what areas that leadership was provided. Other areas of study included school size, socioeconomic status of students, and the district's role in decisions affecting the school.

On-site interviews were conducted in each high school with the principals and four teachers: the English and mathematics department heads and one teacher from each of these departments. Structured interviews were used to collect information on school leadership. Although six leadership areas were examined, only results from the *leading instructional improvement and innovation* and *staff development* areas are cited here.

Three indicators of *instructional improvement* were analyzed:

- Curriculum or instructional innovation led by the principal
- Principal role in decisions on curriculum design and changes in curriculum
- Principal efforts to increase academic learning time during the school day

Table 6.1 displays the frequencies of principal leadership ratings for the categories. Twelve of the thirty-two principals received a high rating for leading some innovation in curriculum or instruction, such as initiating revised courses or introducing new instructional methods. In almost half of the schools (fifteen), ratings on this indicator were mixed; that is,

---

Unlocking Online Resources for Instructional Leaders

Browse the following Web sites for information on standards and curriculum:

- ERIC Database: http://www.eric.ed.gov/. This site puts you in touch with school leaders around the country.
- Assessment and Accountability: http://www.aacompcenter.org. This site provides information about NCLB requirements and resources as regards meeting standards.
- American Federation of Teachers: http://www.aft.org/teachers/index.htm
- Center for Educational Reform: http://edreform.com/standard.htm
- Association for Supervision and Curriculum Development (ASCD): http://www.ascd.org. A subscription to ASCD's ancillary site, "Only the Best Web Site," allows complete access to the most up-to-date version of the ASCD Curriculum Handbook.

Share what you find with colleagues and staff by sending them hyperlinks or by printing out pages where permissible.

Table 6.1 Extent of Principal Leadership in Six Areas

Area of Principal Leadership	Leadership Rating		
Indicator(s)	Low 0–1	Medium 2–3	High 4–5
(1) Instructional Improvement			
Initiated innovation	5	15	12
Decisions on curriculum	19	10	3
Increase academic learning time	1	3	28
(2) Staff Development			
Decisions on staff development	8	15	9
Curriculum & instruction			
in faculty meetings	14	9	9

N = 32 Urban High Schools

Average of five individual responses per school (Low = 10–20%; Medium = 21–30%; High = 38–62%)

Rating = sum of individual responses of principal and four teachers per school (item descriptions noted in the text)

respondents from the same school did not agree that the principal had provided leadership in instructional innovation. The findings for the second item—principal decisions on curriculum—indicate that many of the principals who led instructional innovations did not take a leadership role in deciding on the school curriculum; only three of the thirty-two principals (9 percent) received a high rating, and nineteen (60 percent) received a low leadership rating. A possible explanation is that curriculum is not typically viewed as part of the principal's role. During the interviews, some teachers reported that district administrators and school department heads provided more leadership on curriculum decisions than did principals.

A majority of the principals (28, or 87%) received high ratings for increasing "academic learning time" during class periods and throughout the school day (for instance, by limiting external interruptions of classes, reducing excused absences for special activities, and improving scheduling). This finding may show that urban high schools have responded to the attention focused on the learning time issue and begun to emphasize better use of school time.

There are two indicators of principal leadership in staff development:

- Principal role in decisions on staff development programs
- Proportion of time in faculty meetings spent on curriculum and instruction matters

The principal was highly rated as a leader in making staff development decisions in nine schools (29%). The second indicator—proportion of time in faculty meetings spent on curriculum and instruction matters—was used as a measure of "informal" staff development within the school.

Nine schools spent more than 38% of faculty meeting time on curriculum and instructional matters, while almost half (14 schools) spent less than 20% of time on these issues. These data show that some urban high school principals take advantage of regular monthly meetings to focus on the academic program; this activity is consistent with the effective schools research's emphasis on school-based staff development and instructional improvement.

THREE OVERLAPPING APPROACHES ■

Depending on where one sits, the principal's role as an effective curriculum leader varies. Let us review three overlapping yet distinct qualities from three different advisors: a college professor and senior consultant at a Curriculum Leadership Institute, two school principals, and a college professor who has consulted with more than 100 school systems on curriculum.

In a *Tips for Principals* document for a secondary principals' association, Bailey (1990) cites 12 basic tenets that can be used to guide principals in the role of effective curriculum leaders. A tenet, as defined by Bailey, is an opinion, doctrine, or principle considered to be true.

Tenet No. 1: Curriculum leaders' actions are guided by a curriculum model.

Tenet No. 2: Curriculum leaders use curriculum governance documents to identify and clarify the directions, roles, and responsibilities of all stakeholders in the curriculum construction and curriculum monitoring process.

Tenet No. 3: Curriculum leaders create and use curriculum materials that are tied to school district guiding documents.

Tenet No. 4: Curriculum leaders know the difference between curriculum construction and curriculum monitoring and employ leadership skills according to the state of curriculum work.

Tenet No. 5: Curriculum leaders see curriculum development as a continuous process.

Tenet No. 6: Curriculum leaders believe empowerment is a leadership behavior or characteristic and empower others in curriculum construction and monitoring.

Tenet No. 7: Curriculum leaders see the interconnectedness of curriculum supervision and staff development.

Tenet No. 8: Curriculum leaders are trained, not born. (Administrators, like all personnel, must participate in effective training programs that include information, theory, demonstration, practice, feedback, and coaching.)

Tenet No. 9: Curriculum leaders are guided by research in the decision-making process (especially the school effects), teacher effects research, and school subject-specific research.

Tenet No. 10: Curriculum leadership emerges from the ranks of all the stakeholders in the school district and school building.

Tenet No. 11: Curriculum leaders believe in self-improvement, staff development, and supervision as tools of instructional leadership improvement.

Tenet No. 12: Curriculum leaders operate as facilitators and seek consensus rather than compromise. (p. 2)

SOURCE: Bailey, G. D. 1990. "How to improve curriculum, leadership—Twelve tenets." *Tips for principals for principals,* Jan. 1990. Reston: VA: National Association of Secondary School Principals. Used with permission of NASSP.

■ SUBTLE CLUES

The effective principal will be cognizant of subtle clues that will affect his or her status as instructional leader. In a NASSP collection of selected readings focusing on instructional leadership, Hutto and Criss (1996, pp. 15–18) offer several practical ways principals can improve how others perceive them as instructional leaders.

Look What's Talking—Your Body!

Much research exists about body language and its implications. Has a teacher ever come to you to discuss an instructional matter and not received your full attention because you are distracted by unfinished business on your desk? Come around that desk and sit facing the teacher. Give him or her your full attention. Better yet, arrange to meet in the teacher's classroom during a lunch or planning period.

Top Billing

What's top billing in your school? Ask most principals that question and they will quickly and emphatically answer, "instruction." But how can you make sure that your subtle messages are saying, "Instruction is number one in this school"?

Most schools have a series of morning announcements about activities, awards, and other business. How you order these announcements may send out a signal. Hutto and Criss (1996) advise that announcements about instructional matters (e.g., academic teams, student academic awards, and academic testing dates) be given top billing. By making these announcements first, the principal is saying, albeit subtly, "Instruction is number one in this school."

You Are the Principal Teacher

We know that students learn by example, but so do adults. Faculty meetings are the principal's classroom. Make sure they are well-planned and coordinated. Follow an agenda that allows ample time for questions and comments, but do not waste faculty time with meaningless digressions and ramblings.

The order of the agenda for faculty meetings may convey a message. As with morning announcements, Hutto and Criss (1996) say, give instructional matters top billing. Make sure that instructional items are listed first on your agenda and cover them with enthusiasm and conviction.

Kids Hear the Darndest Things

Most students appreciate positive comments. Congratulatory remarks about academics from the principal do two things: They serve as a motivator for students, and they send a subtle message that the principal really cares about academics.

> **Unlocking Support for Curricular Initiatives**
>
> To develop a culture that supports curriculum work in the school, you must encourage teachers to value curriculum work. This means that you must talk about curriculum continuously, stressing its importance and speaking knowledgeably about general curriculum matters.

All members of the school community take their cues from the principal, Hutto and Criss (1996) point out. Have you noticed that if you "harrumph" through the morning announcements, some student will soon remark about your bad mood? Or if you scowl as you monitor the halls between classes, the janitor will ask you what is wrong? It doesn't take long for your mood to affect a number of people, and they get the idea that school is not a pleasant place in which to spend their time. Face it—there are days when the job gets us down, but the people around us should be the last to know!

In *Developing a Quality Curriculum,* Glatthorn (1994) outlines four leadership tasks for principals when developing the school curriculum (within its school district constraints): developing a culture that supports curriculum work, providing support for curriculum work, performing evaluation functions, and developing school goals and vision. These leadership tasks are equally appropriate for the school principal who chooses to use curriculum as a tool for instructional leadership.

Support involves providing quality time to enable teachers to develop the materials they will need to implement the curriculum effectively (such as yearly planning calendars, sample units, and instructional materials). When you encourage teachers to take risks with curriculum, you reduce the pressure teachers feel regarding their evaluation.

Teams and departments should be encouraged to use planning time for developing curriculum units and learning materials. You might also support the curriculum by working with teachers in planning and implementing staff development needed for effective implementation of the defined curriculum. This is not an unusual task considering the recent state and national adoptions of new standards that drive revised and new curriculum development in most content subjects.

Glatthorn (1994) enumerates several critical evaluation functions that require the principal's leadership and attention.

First, the program of studies for the school needs to be evaluated. Specific suggestions for evaluating the program of studies can be found in Box 6.2.

Second, you should actively monitor the implementation of curricula. Recommended methods include conferring with teachers, talking with students, reviewing test and other performance results, and observing

---

Box 6.2   Criteria for Evaluating a Program of Studies

A sound program of studies is

1. GOAL ORIENTED. The program of studies enables the students to accomplish the district's mastery goals.

2. BALANCED. The program of studies provides an appropriate balance between required courses that ensure mastery of essential knowledge and skills and elective courses that enable students to develop and pursue special interests, and the time allocated to those subjects appropriately reflects the school's curricular priorities.

3. INTEGRATED. The program of studies enables students to understand the interrelationship of knowledge from various disciplines and to use knowledge from several disciplines to examine personal and societal problems.

4. SKILLS REINFORCED. The skills required for learning in many subject areas (writing to learn, reading in the content areas, critical thinking, and learning and studying skills) are given appropriate and timely emphasis.

5. OPEN-ENDED. The program of studies gives all students the knowledge and skills they may need for future success. Students are not tracked into dead-end programs on the basis of premature career choices.

6. RESPONSIVE. The program of studies is responsive to the special needs of the student population served by that school.

---

classes. When you routinely engage in these types of activities, you become aware of developing problems and emerging strengths.

Another key evaluation function is assessing the coordination between levels of schooling. There should be a well-coordinated K–12 program where learning is unaffected by the divisions between levels of schooling. By analyzing test scores, conferring with classroom teachers, and discussing the issue with the principals of sending and receiving schools, you are in a special position to detect problems of level-to-level coordination.

You can lead by assessing the extent to which several curricula are aligned. Curriculum alignment is a process of ensuring that the supported curriculum of texts and other materials and the tested curriculum are congruent with the written curriculum. Alignment strengthens the taught curriculum.

Your leadership is also required in assessing whether the hidden curriculum is congruent with the stated values (yours, other administrators' and teachers,' the school's mission statement). With teachers, you need to systematically examine the impact of such elements as the reward system, the disciplinary policies, the physical environment, and the allocation of funds (Glatthorn, 1994, pp. 67–69).

THE HIDDEN CURRICULUM   ■

Earlier, three types of curriculum were introduced: the written, the taught, and the tested (English, 2000). There are, however, two additional types: the null and the hidden curriculums.

The null curriculum is that which is not in the curriculum. The hidden curriculum is curriculum that is not explicit or of which the participants are unaware. Another definition of the hidden curriculum, offered by Simpson and Erickson (1983), follows:

> The hidden curriculum is the unstated but influential knowledge, attitudes, norms, rules, rituals, values and beliefs that are transmitted to students through structure, policies, processes, formal content, and the social relationship of school. (p. 184)

The following incidental yet pervasive "lessons" that students absorb early in school are examples Aronowitz and Giroux (1993) offer as representative of the hidden curriculum.

1. Teachers are more powerful than students; principals are more powerful than teachers.

2. Some children are called on to perform favors for teachers; others are not.

3. Teachers call on well-dressed children more often than poorly dressed children.

4. Teachers praise boys more than girls.

5. Interruptions and intrusions are frequent and unavoidable.

6. No matter how hard some children try to gain the favor and attention of the teacher, some will never succeed.

7. Teachers behave more favorably toward the children whose parents participate in school activities.

Frequent Curriculum Criticisms

In addition to dealing with the "hidden curriculum," keep in mind three frequently articulated curriculum criticisms:

- Teaching students what they already know while omitting things they should know
- Focusing on the transmission of factual knowledge to the near exclusion of conceptual understanding and problem solving
- Being disconnected from real experiences, authentic writing efforts, real problems of citizenship, serious questions about the Earth's environment, practical uses of mathematical thinking (Gehrke, 1997)

■ CURRICULUM MONITORING

Curriculum monitoring is an evaluation process that asks the question "Are teachers implementing the curriculum with reasonable fidelity?" Such monitoring can seem intrusive at times and can imply a distrust of teachers. Thus, it tends to be a matter of great sensitivity among most teachers. The wise urban school principal, therefore, adheres to the school district's monitoring policy and accompanying procedures uniformly throughout the school.

Consider this strategy to ensure that your assistant principals have an *understanding of the curriculum* for each academic, vocational, career, visual and performing arts, technology, and other curriculum that is monitored. If you have only one assistant principal, you are encouraged to assign the assistant principal 50% of the content areas and take the rest yourself. If you have three assistant principals and there are 10 subject areas taught in the school, two assistant principals would be assigned three disciplines each and one would be assigned four. You would rotate the assignments each year so that over the course of a three year period, each assistant principal would be conversant with each curriculum.

In specifically designed professional development sessions led by you, and with the assistance of district discipline experts (mathematics, science, social studies, etc.), review the curriculums and the timelines to become conversant with the scope and sequence of the content that teachers are expected to cover by grade level and each marking period. You might also develop a quiz that the assistant principal will take for the subject areas that he or she supervises.

By having these discussions and the quizzes, both you and the assistant principals will be better prepared to engage teachers in discussion about what is observed during observations and learning walks. Teachers' receptiveness to administrative suggestions and recommendations will increase. When I did this with the three assistant principals assigned to my school, their initial response was outrage. Three months into the school year, I was thanked repeatedly for having the courage and insight to insist that the assistant principals had a firm curriculum foundation. Four years after leadership development under me, my assistant principals were ready to lead schools of their own.

CURRICULUM REFLECTIVE PRACTICE EXERCISES

Curriculum

Reflective Practice Exercise #1

ENSURING SOUND CURRICULUM/ INSTRUCTIONAL PRACTICES

Determine whether or not the statements that follow accurately reflect your school's attention to the important role curriculum plays in successful learning. For those statements you find do not reflect what your school is currently doing, undertake an action plan in concert with your governing team to appropriately prioritize curriculum.

	Yes	No
All teacher-made tests are checked by the appropriate department head, assistant principal, or principal.	☐	☐
Quarterly grade analysis reports are distributed and discussed with teachers.	☐	☐
All teachers are required to use a variety of teaching techniques that balance teacher-centered and student-centered activities.	☐	☐
The identification and placement of students are appropriate and equitable. Students have flexibility of movement among instructional/academic groups as their skills and interests change. The instructional program for special populations is definable and defensible.	☐	☐

- Special education
- Title I
- Limited English proficient
- Returning students
- Students in need of remediation

The library/media center is an integral component of the school's overall instructional program and plays a key role in developing students' information literacy.	☐	☐

Curriculum

Reflective Practice Exercise #2

STABILIZING SOUND CURRICULUM/ INSTRUCTIONAL PRACTICES

Determine whether or not the statements that follow accurately reflect your school's attention to the important role curriculum plays in successful learning. For those statements you find do not reflect what your school is currently doing, undertake an action plan in concert with your governing team to appropriately prioritize curriculum.

Goal: To establish clear expectations that quality instruction is the school's priority.

	Yes	No
Administrators work cooperatively with teachers and resource personnel in the development of the instructional program.	☐	☐
Administrators work cooperatively with teachers and resource personnel to plan, develop, and encourage professional growth activities for teachers.	☐	☐
Opportunities for inter- and intradisciplinary instruction are created and monitored by school staff and by resource and support personnel.	☐	☐
Administrators interact with students to aid in determining the effect of the instructional program.	☐	☐
Time during the instructional day is available for professional development.	☐	☐
Professional materials, equipment (computers, AV, etc.), and resources are available in the school for professional development for teachers.	☐	☐
Both content and skills are taught in every class.	☐	☐
Preparatory classes are available for students to prepare for and take college entrance tests, PSAT, SAT, and ACT.	☐	☐
A comprehensive preparatory program for college begins in Grades 6 and 9 and informs instruction in all the disciplines.	☐	☐
A study skills course is offered to all sixth- and ninth-grade students (e.g., Content focuses on organizational skills, taking notes, using the computer, vocabulary enrichment, and the development of self-esteem).	☐	☐
Coach classes are conducted by every teacher.	☐	☐
The recognition of excellent teachers is supported and encouraged both formally and informally.	☐	☐

Curriculum

Reflective Practice Exercise #3

SUSTAINING SOUND CURRICULUM/ INSTRUCTIONAL PRACTICES

Determine whether or not the statements that follow accurately reflect your school's attention to the important role curriculum plays in successful learning. For those statements you find do not reflect what your school is currently doing, undertake an action plan in concert with your governing team to appropriately prioritize curriculum.

Goal: To establish clear expectations that equity and access are critical for excellence.

	Yes	No
Teachers are encouraged and rewarded for participating in professional development that increases their skill levels in student learning styles.	☐	☐
Diversity (race/gender/age) is one criterion used for staffing assignments at the team, house, and/or grade level.	☐	☐
In the school action plan, there is a goal for multicultural issues specific to the school's climate and culture needs.	☐	☐

Curriculum

Reflective Practice Exercise #4

Review the last three reflective practice exercises. After checking off those items that you are currently performing to your satisfaction, reread the list. Identify where you want to be in 30-day increments for those items you think will result in significant payoffs (e.g., increased student achievement, curricular unity throughout the school, teacher ownership for student achievement, and a school climate conducive to learning).

Typical questions to use to guide your self-reflection might include these:

- What will we be doing in 30 days that we aren't doing now?

- How about in 60 days? Ninety days?

- What are we doing that we want to keep?

- What are we doing that we want to discard?

- What challenges will we have to overcome?

- What barriers will we still face?

- What skills are we learning?

Develop a plan of action to ensure that ongoing attention to curriculum and instructional practices undergirds the school's overarching goals and mission.

7

Courage

Risk Taking and Responsibility

Reginald Armstrong, a newly assigned urban school principal, was appointed during the summer. As Principal Armstrong walked through his new building for the first time, he noticed that what little furniture there was in the teachers' lounge was worn and mismatched. There wasn't even a work table. After speaking with two teachers, Principal Armstrong decided to conduct an oral needs assessment with every teacher who entered the building during the summer. Predictably, 85% of the staff referred to the teachers' lounge as a priority.

Principal Armstrong contacted staff in the district office to order furniture for the teachers' lounge. He was not successful. So he visited the school district's warehouse and secured furniture, without permission, for the teachers' lounge. His wife decorated the room with pictures, plants, and curtains. The teachers were delighted. The risk for the principal was moving district furniture without proper authorization. This principal took a risk to satisfy the needs of his customers, the teachers.

■ LEARNING TO TAKE RISKS AS A SCHOOL LEADER

One requirement you have as a newly assigned or appointed principal is to take calculated risks to implement strategies and procedures to improve student achievement. When you do this, conflicts will arise. In fact, you should understand that conflict is built into the very fabric of the school regardless of what you do. This conflict can sap the morale of the institution, or it can be an asset. Properly managed, it can help set the stage for challenge and change. It can inspire creativity, raise alternative solutions, redirect efforts, clarify goals and expectations, and eliminate unnecessary work. It can energize and motivate people, provide them with a positive group identity, and increase trust within an organization. In short, conflict can *work for you* in a changing world. But unless you manage conflict successfully, you're in a no-win situation—even if it may, for a time, feel like you've won.

This chapter is about having the courage to take risks and managing conflict through balance—the balance between caring and accountability, between support and constructive criticism, between organizational loyalty and truth, between substance and style, between leading and listening. It is balanced management that allows us to use conflict without allowing it to turn into warfare.

■ DON'T BE AFRAID TO FAIL

In sports, there is an expression that propels athletes to both practice and take risks: "You miss 100% of the shots you never take." In the state of Maryland, the slogan for the state lottery is "You've got to play to win." If you do not buy a lottery ticket, you cannot win the large sums of money awarded each day. Implicit in these two guideposts for chance taking is the message that "not failure, but low aim, is sin."

Educators often confuse risk and danger; consequently, many educational leaders are reluctant to take risks. This is because our language confuses danger with the possibilities of embarrassment or disapproval that risk entails. When considering a risky initiative, some people, according to Wallace Wilkins (1999a), automatically imagine physical harm:

"If I tried that, she'd rip my head off."

"If I'm not careful, he'll tear me limb from limb!"

"I would just die."

"I'd fall to pieces."

"He'll explode."

Can you think of similar expressions? If you color your anticipation of the future with alarming thoughts, you will automatically inhibit your action. However, those alarms are false alarms.

There is risk when an outcome is uncertain. There is danger when you experience harm, physical or otherwise. Some initiatives succeed. Some don't. The risk of failure or embarrassment does not make the future dangerous. You will not be physically harmed during most changes. Each time you do something new or different, you confront a risk. The kinds of risk-taking advocated here should not precipitate potential bodily harm to you as a leader. If you determine that danger is not likely, then evaluate the evidence concerning future outcomes. You don't have to be certain about an outcome to take action.

PLAN, DO, STUDY, ACT ■

Instead of following a pattern of plan-plan-plan-plan-plan-fail, successful companies today are following a course of try, test, fix it, try it again, adjust it (Peters & Waterman, 2004). They are building a style that makes room for learning from one's errors instead of seeing them as a statement of one's inadequacy.

Unlocking the Courage to Fail

Consider placing the following anonymous statement in your planning document as well as in your wallet. When you feel especially challenged, read the statement aloud three times. I guarantee that you will brush yourself off and begin again with enthusiasm!

Don't be afraid to fail. You've failed many times, although you may not remember. You fell down the first time you tried to walk. You almost drowned the first time you tried to swim, didn't you? Did you hit the ball the first time you swung a bat? Heavy hitters, the ones who hit the most home runs, also strike out a lot. R. H. Macy failed seven times before his store in New York caught on. English novelist John Creasy got 753 rejection slips before he published 564 books. Babe Ruth struck out 1,330 times, but he also hit 714 home runs.

Don't worry about failure. Worry about chances you miss when you don't even try.

YIN YANG: A PERSPECTIVE FOR RISK TAKING ■

The ancient Confucian tradition is one John Jay Bonstingl (2001) recommends for leaders who lead with purpose. Graphically, the Confucian tradition is represented by the yin yang symbol, an ancient Oriental symbol of wholeness, shown below.

The yin yang symbol is divided into two parts. Each half depends upon the other half for its existence. Neither has meaning without the other. Nothing can exist without its opposite. To know good is impossible without knowing evil. To know what is wrong, one must also know what is right. Each element is balanced by its opposite. Life consists not of adversarial dichotomies but of *dualities*—polar opposites that add richness and meaning to one another.

Notice that within the light half of the yin yang symbol there is a dark dot, and within the dark half there is a light dot of the same size. This signifies that everything contains a small element of its opposite. In the evil that befalls each of us there are the seeds of good. From death springs life;

Figure 7.1   Yin Yang

from endings come beginnings. Thus, life is viewed as a cycle or spiral, a continuous wheel of existence known to the people of India as the Great Mandala. Life in the Eastern tradition is one cloth, never ending and interconnected.

Knowledge about your attitude toward risk taking should prove to be most helpful as you lead or retreat from leadership. The Courage Reflective Practice Exercise #1 will help with this.

■ BUILD AWARENESS

In whatever initiative you decide to implement, the focus should be threefold: focusing first on your own awareness and readiness; then on that of your subordinates; and last but not least, on the community with whom you work.

Faculty, Staff, and Students

There are many strategies you might implement with your faculty and staff to determine their readiness for change. Keep in mind that the strategies will require that you take some level of risk. These strategies are recommended here because it is a given that your first year in the school will be filled with surprises!

Conduct Faculty and Staff Interviews

Is the school faculty and staff ready for change? How do you determine a staff's readiness? You may be an administrator who has been fortunate enough to handpick the "new" faculty for your school, and you and your team are of one accord regarding short- and long-range plans. If this is not your scenario, you can increase your risk taking effectiveness by interviewing faculty and staff, individually, in teams, by departments, and in small groups. The data you collect from this process *supplements the other data* that you might have been given about factors such as student achievement, attendance, participation in cocurricular options, and staff attendance. This data collection process gives *voice* to teachers. Research shows that if teachers are not informed and active participants, reform efforts will fail (ERS, 2000). Ask these three questions:

- What three things do this faculty and staff do well? How do you know this?
- What do you like most about working in this school?
- If you could change three things in this school, what would you change?

Note that what some people say is an asset, others will describe as a liability. This will be noted in your written summary of the interviews.

You can use the data you collect in a variety of ways. To avoid being overly prescriptive, let's leave those decisions to your best judgment. However, you should summarize the data, both graphically and in a narrative report, and share it with the faculty and staff within the first month of school. Based on your findings, you might assign the report to an existing committee to do something with the "things faculty and staff do well."

> ### Unlocking Your Tolerance for Risk
>
> Where are you on a continuum of risk tolerance? Are you a T-Bill Leader or a Small Stocks Leader willing to assertively move forward with new initiatives with less than 50% of the faculty and staff in your corner? Do you need positive reinforcement from your boss before moving forward? How do you make use of data that will support moving ahead to increase student achievement when there is a staff actively engaged in "blaming the victim" for his or her lack of increased academic achievement?

Engage in Small Talk

In *In Search of Excellence*, Peters and Waterman (2004) describe the concept of "inconveniencing oneself." This concept may take many forms, including the one advocated here, which focuses on communication: Management by Walking Around (MBWA). A walk around the school once in the morning and once in the afternoon does wonders for increasing communication between you and individual teachers, the librarian, custodians, the school nurse, cafeteria workers, and other staff members. Learn to master the art of timely small talk as you wander.

If people are truly your most important resource, you must make yourself accessible to them. Some experts suggest that up to 30% of the effective manager's time is spent on such visibility functions. Building common ground through small talk should never take a large amount of your time, but a small investment in cordiality can often pay healthy dividends in cooperation.

Conduct Student Interviews

Students are seldom-used allies. Students are a powerful constituent group, whether they are primary, elementary, middle level, or high school students. Students' parents listen to them, and they act on what they hear. Suppose six students go home and say to their parents or guardians, "Today the principal screamed at our class for no reason." You can count on at least four telephone calls before you leave school for home! Why not take a risk and interview students daily? Think about the powerful messages you can send to parents using this communication tool! Students will become your home ambassadors.

Interview a student each day for the first 60 school days. By doing this, you become better acquainted with students. You learn about their families, hobbies, and attitudes toward life. You also learn what they like and dislike about school.

To become comfortable with interviewing students, interview three students the first day and compare the answers they give to the questions below. You are not limited to these questions; in fact, you will probably be better off if you develop your own questions because every school is unique.

- What do you like best about this school? Why?
- If you could change three things about this school, what would you change and why?
- Who is the one adult in this school who will listen to you if you have a problem?
- Do you feel comfortable talking to teachers about your problems? Why, or why not?
- Is there one teacher in this school who knows you well? Who is this teacher?
- If you ask your teachers, are they willing to help you outside of class time?
- Do you get along well with people who are different from you?
- When you have a complaint or problem, whom do you go to? Is it a teacher, the social worker, the nurse, an assistant principal, the principal, another student?

Community Awareness

How *ready* is your community: parents, volunteers, the school's business partners, the social service agencies' personnel who provide services to students? How do you know this? Who will get angry if criteria for participation in athletics change? Who will get angry if the band is not allowed to perform during the Christmas holiday? To determine your community's awareness level, use the same three questions used earlier with the faculty and staff.

- What three things does this school do well? How do you know this?
- What do you like most about working/volunteering/partnering with/in this school?
- If you could change three things in this school, what would you change?

The principal who preceded you may or may not have managed by walking around. Management by walking around the building is a very specific task. When you make this special effort to be in the halls, especially between classes, the tone and tenor of the school is changed. Initially, students and teachers might not receive you well, but in the long run, both will embrace your presence.

ENCOURAGING OTHERS TO ABANDON THE KNOWN

If your urban school is to remain an intellectually "fun" place to be and student achievement is to be sustained at high levels, it becomes imperative that the school family continually generates new ideas. Here are some techniques that can help.

Think the Unthinkable

In 1987, General Foods, Procter & Gamble, and Nestlé owned nearly 90% of the U.S. coffee market. They didn't worry about the possibility of start-up companies taking away a large share of their market. It was unthinkable that David could possibly beat Goliath.

While the big three conducted business as usual, Starbucks recognized and capitalized on the fact that customer priorities were changing. For a long time the priority was price; what the big three failed to recognize, however, was that customers were willing to spend up to twice as much for gourmet coffee. The new priority was quality, and Starbucks cashed in.

By 1993, Starbucks and similar roasters jointly owned 22% of the national coffee market, worth about $1 billion. General Foods, Procter & Gamble, and Nestlé had a lot of unhappy bean counters.

To get your faculty and staff to think the unthinkable, try asking "What if?" questions. Here are some examples:

- What if a charter school opened in your neighborhood and its students' academic achievement began to far exceed that of your students?
- What if parents were given vouchers to enroll their children in school? Would your school become a school of choice?
- What if the school district provided free transportation for all students to the schools of their choice?
- What if the faculty decided that every student in the school would take one field trip a month to some culturally enriching institution?

When you do nothing, you learn nothing. But when you try and fail, you learn what doesn't work. *So, fail more to succeed more.* Negative feedback provides you with the opportunity to try a different approach. It doesn't matter how often you fail. It matters how often you succeed. Successful salespeople hear "No" far more often than their unsuccessful counterparts simply because they knock on more doors. As a result, they also hear "Yes" far more often. Too many educators blame students and their families for students' failure to excel academically. This attitude is an example of "playing it safe." If you wait until it is safe to act, the charter school competition will beat you to the punch.

Dare to Break the Rules

Pioneer thinkers often create new ideas by breaking the rules. Progress in every trade, field, and discipline occurred when some great

Unlocking Techniques for Academic Achievement

Think of at least five reasons students' academic achievement is not progressing at an acceptable pace in your school. Using the three techniques just listed, think the unthinkable to get back on track! Here are five statements of conditions to get you started.

- Forty percent of fifth, seventh, or ninth graders in your school have repeated two grades. These students' attendance is poor, and they are discipline problems for their teachers.
- On any given school day, 10% of the students arrive late to school.
- Twenty-five percent of the faculty is not certified in the subjects they are assigned to teach.
- The heating and cooling system in the school is constantly broken. This means that people are constantly griping. They are either too hot or too cold.
- Twenty-five percent of the student population has been identified as needing special education services.

independent thinker questioned the status quo. Instead of doing things the same old way, these pioneers made breakthroughs by trying a different approach. What if you decided to eliminate suspensions as a method of discipline in your school? Would the teachers' union file a grievance? Would someone report you to the superintendent and the school board for not suspending students in keeping with school board policy? What if you and your faculty decided that every student would have several shadowing experiences—spending a day with an architect, a carpenter, or the city manager in your city? What if you decided that you would move your desk to the main hall, and there you would work and transact business? Do you suppose students would often stop at your desk? Do you suppose you could get to know every student by name if you did this?

Steve Jobs, George Eastman, and Isaac Singer broke the rules that said computers, cameras, and sewing machines couldn't be designed for home use and mass marketed to the consumer. Fred Smith broke the rule that permitted only the U.S. Post Office to deliver mail in this country: He founded Federal Express.

Rules can sometimes become invisible boundaries that imprison your creative thinking. When you challenge them, you expand your possibilities and come up with more ideas. You become free to look for answers outside the box.

One technique for breaking the rules is to repeat the question "Why?" several times in a row. First, state a rule that's confining your problem. Then ask "Why is this a rule?" When you get an explanation, ask "Why?" again, and then again. This technique prevents you from being satisfied with the standard explanation and enables you to look at rules in a different way.

Breaking the rules is not easy. When you see what others don't see, it takes a tremendous amount of self-confidence and inner strength to ignore critics and pursue your vision. Critics are comfortable with the status quo and afraid of the changes that new ideas bring about. Expect to be criticized when you break the rules, but don't take it personally.

■ THINK LIKE A GENIUS

If you are going to succeed as an urban school principal, you want to think and apply strategies like a genius. How do geniuses come up with ideas?

What is common to the thinking style that produced Mona Lisa, as well as the one that spawned the theory of relativity? What characterizes the thinking strategies of Einstein, Edison, da Vinci, Picasso, Michelangelo, Freud, and Mozart? What can we learn from them?

According to Michael Michalko (1998), eight strategies are common to the thinking styles of creative geniuses in science, art, and industry throughout history.

1. Geniuses look at problems in many different ways.

2. Geniuses make their thoughts visible.

3. Geniuses produce.

4. Geniuses make novel combinations.

5. Geniuses force relationships.

6. Geniuses think in opposites.

7. Geniuses think metaphorically.

8. Geniuses prepare themselves for chance.

An example of three of the above strategies is provided to whet your appetite.

Unlocking Positive Discipline

Disciplining students for inappropriate behavior is a typical problem in urban schools. Think of at least 10 ways a social worker/psychologist/Sunday school teacher might discipline a student. Now select the five least punitive ways among these. How would you measure the effectiveness of the approaches? When teachers complain about your discipline of students, why not use this strategy with teachers to identify the least punitive but effective ways to correct students' inappropriate behavior? The same strategy may be used with teachers working in teams.

Geniuses Look at Problems in Many Different Ways

Genius often comes from finding a new perspective that no one else has taken. In order to solve a problem creatively, the thinker must abandon the initial approach, which stems from past experience, and reconceptualize the problem. By not settling for one perspective, geniuses do not merely solve existing problems, such as inventing an environment-friendly fuel.

Geniuses Produce

A distinguishing characteristic of genius is immense productivity. Bach wrote a cantata every week, even when he was sick or exhausted. Mozart produced more than 600 pieces of music. Edison held 1,093 patents, still the record. He guaranteed productivity by giving himself and his assistants idea quotas. His own personal quota was one minor invention every 10 days and a major invention every six months.

Unlocking Ways to Improve Student Literacy

Think of three ways you might motivate your staff to habitually think of ways to increase students' ability to read daily and to comprehend what they read.

Geniuses Prepare Themselves for Chance

Whenever we attempt to do something and fail, we end up doing something else. That is the first principle of creative accident. We may ask ourselves why we have failed to do what we intended, which is a reasonable question. But the creative accident provokes a different question: *What have we done?*

> **Unlocking Avenues to Creative Insight**
>
> When you have failed to do something as you had hoped and planned, take time to ask, "What have I done?" When you do, you are on your way to creative insight.

Answering that question in a novel, unexpected way is the essential creative act. It is not luck but creative insight of the highest order. According to Michalko (1998), B. F. Skinner emphasized the first principle of scientific methodologists: When you find something interesting, drop everything else and study it. Too many fail to answer opportunity's knock at the door because they have to finish some preconceived plan. Creative geniuses do not wait for the gifts of chance; instead, they actively seek the accidental discovery.

■ CELEBRATE EXCELLENCE

The adults (teachers, counselors, administrators, social workers, psychologists, nurses, instructional aides, custodians, secretaries, etc.) who have chosen to work with you to educate economically poor students deserve to be challenged to problem solve in creative ways because the problems the students bring to the school are unique. You will enhance the staff's feelings of competency and satisfaction when you consistently use the following strategies with them (and require staff to use the strategies independently of you). They result in positive outcomes. It is important that you keep a list of the many positive outcomes the staff achieves in its journey toward excellence. Periodic (quarterly) celebrations of these feats should be part of your calendar.

■ REMOVING OBSTACLES TO ENSURE INCREASED STUDENT ACHIEVEMENT

There are seven bad habits that keep people from thinking creatively about problems in work and life. These mistakes are embedded, especially, in the organizational culture of urban schools and in our individual training as school principals and former teachers. Even though you may not think of your urban school as the place for constant creativity, this philosophy is espoused here because it is so easy to get in a rut and do things because "that is the way we have always done things around here." Your school needs to be a hotbed of creativity as you push for excellence and achieve high expectations. You need to jettison these seven bad habits: failure to ask questions, failure to record ideas, failure to revisit ideas, failure to think in new ways, failure to wish for more, failure to try being creative, failure to tolerate creative behavior.

Obstacle: Failure to Ask Questions

Unless you ask lots of "Why?" questions, you won't generate creative insights—insights you will need to propel your school's science test scores 20 to 25 points, or to reduce the dropout rate by 30%, or to increase parent involvement by 40%! To avoid this most common creativity error, be sure to critique your behavior. Don't take anything for granted, especially success.

At every faculty meeting I conducted the 10 years I was a principal, I always made it a point to ask for creative ideas. The last agenda item was "what if" and/or "other." Many principals value faculty meetings as the one opportunity they have to cultivate a formal, professional atmosphere that is combined with a structured conversation that keeps people "on track" or "focused." Yet, invariably, there is an agenda topic in which creative thinking is in order. Moreover, why meet in the first place if not to take advantage of the group's unique creative potential? One person's question or comment can easily stimulate another's imagination—if you ask for imaginative thinking. Thus, no faculty meeting should reach its end without the leader asking for creative ideas. If you cannot imagine an agenda item for which a "Why?" question would be appropriate, add this item to each month's agenda, and allow teachers to pose two or three questions that relate to students' underachievement (e.g., Why do we group students the way we do? Why are the class periods the length they are? Why do we have recess when we do? Why are parent conferences conducted the way they are? Why do we have PTA meetings at our school? Would we get more parent participation if we held PTA meetings in another or several other locations?). See what happens!

Obstacle: Failure to Record Ideas

Failure to record ideas is a really big problem. Often no one takes minutes of team, department, group, and faculty meetings at which important topics are discussed. Because of this, hundreds of good ideas have simply been forgotten. They have not been recorded. Granted, not all of the ideas at these meetings were good ideas, but in the world of creativity, there's no such thing as a bad idea.

As you think of an "idea bank," consider the analogy of having blocks to build a house or some other object. The more blocks you have and the more varied they are, the more things you can make, and you don't toss out the blocks you haven't used today because you never know what you'll want or need to build tomorrow. If your teams and committees do not record their ideas, they are throwing out valuable assets by throwing out the "unused blocks." If someone had only kept a simple card file of each and every idea, problem-solving sessions on previously discussed topics would be more efficient and maybe more productive.

If you keep a record of your ideas, then when you need new ideas, you can start by reexamining the old ones. Some ideas that seemed crazy three years ago might now be viable. Others might always be crazy, but they might serve as the spark you need to come up with more valuable concepts. (See the Unlocking the Power of Your Great Ideas strategy.)

Unlocking the Power of Your Great Ideas

Writing or journaling your ideas is an important practice for you as an individual as well as for the organization. Keep a log or file of ideas. Teams could create "idea boards" in their team areas. Both students and adults could record ideas concerning a specific topic for a specified period of time. The ideas would be transcribed, reviewed, and implemented as appropriate. This strategy could be used for any organized group in the school. For your personal use as the principal, you might record your ideas in a notebook or journal, use a pocket message recorder, or use e-mail. Of course, you can also come up with your own approach to capturing ideas—something new and creative!

Countless ideas occur to you each month, but many are lost. If you just double the number you save, your raw material for your school's improvement will be enriched by 100%.

Obstacle: Failure to Revisit Ideas

One way to revisit old ideas is to schedule a little time for rambling through the debris of past projects. Every month or two, give yourself an hour to dig out old reports, peek into old working files, and leaf through old appointment books—whatever is necessary to resurface old ideas and bring into focus the context of prior decisions.

Most schools have powerful social mechanisms working against revisiting. You and your assistant principals don't want your past decisions questioned. Team leaders/department heads/grade-level chairs don't want to put an item back on the agenda they managed to get off it last month. Teachers inevitably resist the feeling of backward motion that a reexamination of ideas brings with it. Add to that the danger of someone using revisiting as an excuse for playing the "blame game," and you may find that revisiting causes a level of anxiety that hinders productivity.

In such a case, you have to sell the idea of revisiting before it can be practiced successfully in your school. That's a lengthy process, as is any that requires a change of habit by those in leadership roles. In the meantime, however, you can begin to practice revisitation on your own. Like other creativity practices, this can be done alone or in groups. If enough people become "closet creators" in your school, the organizational change is sure to follow.

Obstacle: Failure to Think in New Ways

You don't get out of the box by doing what you've always done. If you usually sit down and write a list of pros and cons before adopting an alternative, then you have to try a new thinking strategy to come up with anything creative. Get rid of that pro and con analysis as quickly as possible. (Of course, if you have never used a pro and con analysis, then by all means give it a try.)

Visual thinking is usually a good choice. Draw a diagram or picture of the problem you're working on, or think up visual analogies by asking yourself to name five things the problem looks like. Then seek ways to generate fresh perspective by analyzing these images: Ask yourself why the problem looks like that thing. Figure 7.2 is an example of what a picture of a problem might look like.

Figure 7.2   Obstacles to Success

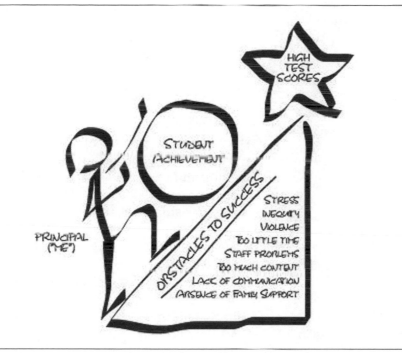

Obstacle: Failure to Wish for More

Creativity is nurtured by optimistic speculation: "Wonder if we could solve that problem?" "Wish there was some way to do that." The failure to wish for more—for the currently unattainable—is a common way to mess up creativity.

Inventors, it seems, are like ordinary people in all respects but one: They always wish there were a better way. When they tie their shoes, they wish they didn't have to tie them, so they think of using buckles, snaps, elastic, Velcro, or magnets. When they think of coloring their nails, they think of 20 different shades of nail polish, designs for each nail, and different lengths for each nail. When they return to their office and listen to their voice mail, they wish there were some way they could avoid missing important messages, so they develop pagers. All innovations arise from the wish to improve upon the status quo.

Yet it is far too easy for us to fall into the routine of our work and slowly lose the knack of wishful thinking. It seems that life is lived at too fast a pace for such habits to persist unless we recognize their value and make a special practice of them. Most of us don't stop to think that wishful thinking is, in fact, a very valuable thing.

Obstacle: Failure to Try Being Creative

Many people feel they are not creative and therefore don't try to be. They don't see how simple it is: You are creative if you engage in creative thinking, and you aren't creative if you don't. Failing to try is the quickest way to derail your creativity. Fortunately, a little effort is the easiest way to get it back on track.

Unlocking Creative Problem Solving

If teachers are not allowed to pilot ideas they have about how to get students to learn concepts and ideas, then they will not be receptive to "What if?" and "Why?" sessions at your faculty meetings. If you communicate a "keep to the script" policy message when you do not see teachers producing something tangible, when and where can the teacher experiment?

Your school cannot profit from teachers' creative potential until you encourage and ask for creativity. Their creativity harnessed and focused on increased student achievement will lead to school accolades and waiting lists for motivated parents and students who want to enroll in your urban school!

Obstacle: Failure to Tolerate Creative Behavior

When people are being creative, sometimes their behavior seems a bit weird to others. Therefore, tolerance of creative behavior—yours and others'—is a must if you want to profit from creative thinking.

Your school will not remain vibrant and student achievement will not be long lasting if you do not collaborate with, coach and mentor, and induct new faculty and staff with the school's mission and vision. How is this done? Consider these strategies:

- Periodic study groups on topics especially challenging as regards advancing student achievement, for example, poor attendance, social-emotional needs of students, violence in the community that spills over into the school, poverty, students' developmental assets, impacting positively on increasing students' aspiration of what happens at the next level (middle school, high school, college).
- Collaboration with teachers by grade level, by department, and with the teacher advisory group as well as with counselors, other certificated staff, and classified staff is central to exhibiting courageous behavior. Implementing staff members' ideas and experiences ensures a level of "buy in" that is needed for institutionalization of critical initiatives.
- Mentoring and coaching of the teaching staff by their peers and others external to the building, followed by recognition in meetings, in e-mails, in the school's newsletter, and in individual memos to the staff, will advance increased student achievement.
- Induction of new faculty in planned ways (reduced teaching load the first semester, assignment of a buddy teacher, assignment of a mentor teacher, intra-school classroom observations followed by debriefing sessions, extra assistance for first parent-teacher conference, etc.) will demonstrate thinking outside the box.

By using the strategies suggested herein, you will be reframing issues that, at first blush, appear to be intractable. No problem is insurmountable. With a little courage, teamwork, and determination, a person can overcome most challenges. Indeed, John C. Maxwell was accurate in his observation that "Coming together is a beginning. Keeping together is progress. Working together is success." Success is what urban school leaders attain when they systematically employ the seven Keys to Success discussed in this book.

COURAGE REFLECTIVE PRACTICE EXERCISES

Courage

Reflective Practice Exercise #1

You must begin with yourself by assessing your personal comfort with taking risks; learning new material, strategies, and procedures; and using new tools to assess effectiveness. An analogy that comes to mind is the one financial planners use when they consult with you to determine your level of risk taking (see Figure 7.3).

Investors are given options that require them to assess their comfort with fluctuation and volatility. Diversity in one's portfolio further complicates the options. Consider this continuum:

RISK AND POTENTIAL REWARD

```
          MMA      STBA              IVA      LVE           SVEA
_____1_____2_____3____4_____5_____
Low                                                                    High

        T-Bill     Bond Index    S & P        Small Stocks
                                 500
```

Type	Risk Acceptability
Money Market Account	People who are looking for a temporary "holding place" are uncomfortable with a great deal of fluctuation in their account value.
Short-Term Bond Account	People who want to diversify their portfolio but are uncomfortable with a great deal of fluctuation in their account.
International Value Account	People who are willing to tolerate fluctuations in their account value in exchange for potentially higher long-term returns.
Large Value Equity	People seeking long-term growth of capital. People with a long-term investment horizon.
Small Growth Equity	People who are willing to tolerate fluctuations in their account value in exchange for potentially higher long-term (five- to ten-year) returns. People who want to diversify their portfolio through investing in an aggressive equity account.

Figure 7.3   Risk Taking Flow Chart

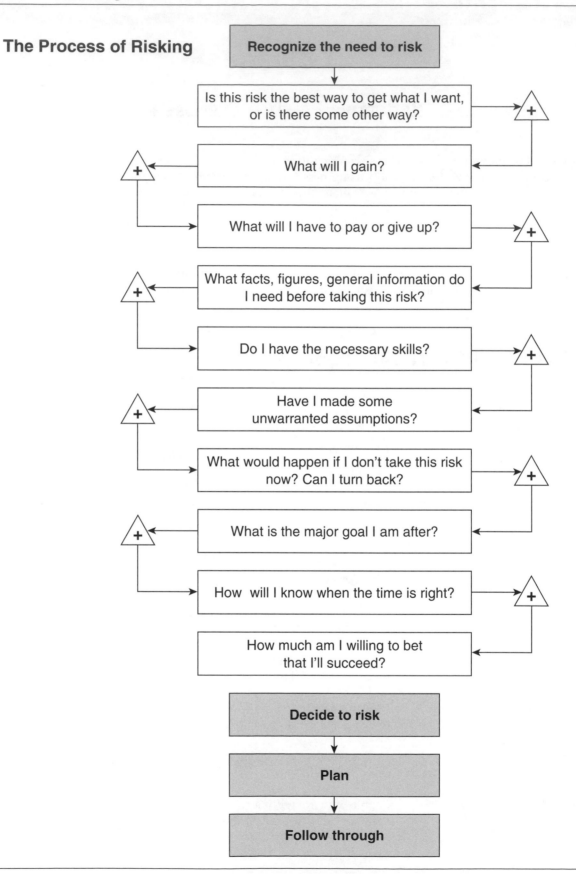

Courage

Reflective Practice Exercise #2

Consider sharing this self-assessment with your mentor or a colleague you trust. Begin systematically addressing each self-handicap so that you are more comfortable with taking risks to advance students' increased academic achievement.

AM I HANDICAPPING MYSELF?

Checklist of possible reasons for self-handicapping, which inhibits assertive, creative, responsible leadership.

Check all that apply to you as an urban school principal.

1. _____ I do not attempt because I would risk failing.

   _____ I might look foolish.

   _____ Other people might laugh and ridicule me.

2. _____ I do not attempt because I might be punished.

3. _____ I do not attempt because I would risk succeeding.

   _____ I might get additional responsibilities.

   _____ Other people would get the credit.

4. _____ I do not attempt because I do not deserve success.

   _____ I am unworthy of success.

   _____ I have not earned success.

   _____ I have not worked hard enough yet.

5. _____ I do not attempt because it would be selfish of me.

6. _____ I do not attempt because I do not have permission.

7. _____ I do not attempt because other people would be distressed with me.

   _____ They might be disappointed in me.

   _____ They might feel threatened.

8. _____ I do not attempt because I might lose control.

9. _____ I do not attempt because I don't know how.

Courage

Reflective Practice Exercise #3

How might you, as an urban school principal, translate the characteristics of a growing small town to the operation of your school? The list below summarizes Cornelia Flora's research on why some small towns grow while others fail (Flora & Flora, 1989). The eight distinguishing characteristics illustrate that a communication paradigm, undergirded by shared decision making and shared accountability, results in productivity and progress.

Take each declarative statement and make it a question about the faculty and staff at your school. The first statement as a question would be "To what extent is controversy considered a normal part of participatory governance in my school?" List the names of staff members for whom this is true. Rephrase other statements and assess how your faculty and staff are operating using a scale of one to five.

Complete the same exercise using the statements under "Dying Small Towns."

LESSONS FOR URBAN PRINCIPALS FROM SMALL TOWN EXPERIENCES

Growing Small Towns

- Controversy was considered a normal part of participatory governance.
- People held an objective view of politics.
- The emphasis in schools was on academics.
- There was a willingness to tax themselves.
- There was a willingness to risk for the good of the town.
- The town had the ability to expand; a place was made for more people.
- People networked horizontally as well as vertically.
- People were flexible. Community leadership was dispersed.

SOURCE: North Central Regional Center for Rural Development, 1988. "Characteristics of Entrepreneurial Communities in a Time of Crisis." *Rural Development News* 12:2 (April 1988), pp. 1–4.

Dying Small Towns

- People avoided controversy and refused to address issues.
- People personalized their politics. They couldn't separate the person from the job.
- Schools tried to hold people's interests by promoting loyalty to sports.
- The leadership identified needs, but they were not willing to tax themselves for gain.
- There was stagnation.
- Citizens refused to share power and authority with newcomers.
- Citizens refused to learn from anyone who wasn't exactly like them.
- Leadership was in the hands of one person.

Resources

*School Leadership
Styles Instruments*

Leadership Styles Instruments

Instrument	Focus	Type	Admin. Time	Scoring	(1) Score Interpretation	(2) Reliability	(3) Validity	Availability
EDUCATION SPECIFIC								
Administrator Perceiver Interview (1979)	Administrator functions, rapport with staff, effect on school climate	Interview	60 minutes	Hand—Requires trained interviewers	Fair-Good Requires trained interviewers	Good	Fair-Good	Selection Research, Inc. PO Box 5700 Lincoln, NE 68505
Educational Administrator Effectiveness Profile (1984)	Administrative behavior	Self-report Other report	30 minutes	Hand	Excellent	Fair-Good	Fair	American Association of School Administrators 1801 N. Moore St., Arlington, VA 22209 (or) Association for Supervision and Curriculum Development 125 N. West St. Alexandria, VA 22314
Leadership Skills Inventory (1985)	Ages 10 to adult: Administration and leadership skills and traits	Self-report	45 minutes	Hand	Fair	Good-Excellent	Fair-Good	D.O.K. Publishers PO Box 605 East Aurora, NY 14052
NASSP Assessment Center (1985)	Administration and leadership skills; traits of K–12 principals	Performance	2 days	Hand—Requires trained observers	Excellent— Requires trained observers	Excellent	Fair-Good	NASSP 1904 Associate Dr., Reston, VA 22091

Leadership Styles Instruments (Continued)

Instrument	Focus	Type	Admin. Time	Scoring	(1) Score Interpretation	(2) Reliability	(3) Validity	Availability
EDUCATION SPECIFIC (Continued)								
Profile of a School: Staff Questionnaire (1986)	Administrator style—authoritarian, benevolent, authoritarian consultative or participative	Student, staff, parent, school board, and superintendent effectiveness questionnaire	40 minutes	Machine	Good	Good-Excellent	Good	Rensis Liker Associates Wolverine Tower 3001 S.State St., Suite 401, Ann Arbor, MI 48108
GENERAL ACROSS BUSINESS AND INDUSTRY								
Human Resources Development Report (1987)	Leadership style and traits	Self-report	45 minutes	Machine	Excellent	Fair-Good	Good	Institute for Personality and Ability Testing PO Box 188 Champaign, IL 61820
Leader Behavior Analysis II (1985)	Leadership style	Self-report Associate report Subordinate report	20 minutes	Hand	Good	Fair	Fair	Blanchard Training and Development, Inc. 125 State Place Escondido, CA 92025
Leader Behavior Questionnaire (1938)	Leader effectiveness	Self-report Associate report	20 minutes	Hand	Excellent	Fair	Good	Organization Design and Development 2002 Renaissance Boulevard King of Prussia, PA 19406

Leadership Styles Instruments   (Continued)

GENERAL ACROSS BUSINESS AND INDUSTRY

Instrument	Focus	Type	Admin. Time	Scoring	(1) Score Interpretation	(2) Reliability	(3) Validity	Availability
Leadership Behavior Description Questionnaire (1963)	Leadership styles— Consideration and initiating structure	Self-report Subordinate report Superior report	20 minutes	Hand	Fair	Fair-Good	Fair	Dr. Randy Babbitt Dept. of Management and Organization College of Bus. Administration Ohio State University Columbus, OH 43210 Barbara Roach (614) 292-9301
Leadership Opinion Questionnaire (1969)	Leadership styles— Consideration and structure	Self-report	15 minutes	Hand	Fair-Good	Good	Good	SRA Inc. 155 N. Wacker Dr., Chicago, IL 60606
Leadership Practices Inventory (1988)	Leadership behavior Leadership activities	Self-report Subordinate Report	15 minutes	Hand	Good	Good-Excellent	Good-Excellent	University Associates, Inc. 8517 Production Ave., San Diego, CA 92121
Least Preferred Coworker Scale (1967)	General leadership style	Self-rate Questionnaire	5 minutes	Hand	Good	Good	Good	F. E. Fiedler, Dept. of Psychology University of Washington Seattle, WA 98195 (206)543-2640
Management Style Diagnostic Test (1973)	Managerial style Managerial effectiveness	Self-report	30 minutes	Hand	Good	Not given	Not given	Organization Test Ltd. Box 324 Fredericton, NB Canada E3B 4Y9

Leadership Styles Instruments (Continued)

Instrument	Focus	Type	Admin. Time	Scoring	(1) Score Interpretation	(2) Reliability	(3) Validity	Availability
GENERAL ACROSS BUSINESS AND INDUSTRY (Continued)								
Managerial Philosophies Scale (1986)	Leadership style—Theory X & Y	Self-report	?	Hard	Fair	Good	Fair	Teleometrics
Multifactor Leadership Questionnaire- From 5 (1989)	Leadership types Leadership behavior	Self-report Subordinate report	20 minutes	Hard	Good	Good	Good	Consulting Psychologists Press 577 College Ave. Palo Alto, CA 94306
Myers-Briggs (1983)	Leadership style	Self-report Personality	60 minutes	Hand/machine	Good	Fair-Good	Good	Consulting Psychologists Press 577 College Ave. Palo Alto, CA 94306
Nelson-Valenti Self-Scoring Survey of Education Leadership (1979)	Leadership style— Bureaucratic, technocratic, idiocratic, democratic	Self-report	30–45 minutes	Hand	Fair-Good	Fair-Good	Good	Management Research Assoc RR 25, Box 26 Terre Haute, IN 47802
Situational Leadership (1979–82)	Leadership style—Match to employee needs Consideration and initiative structure	Self-report Subordinate report Observation	?	Hand	Fair	Not given	None given	University Associates, Inc. 8517 Production Ave., San Diego, CA 92121

131

Leadership Styles Instruments   (Continued)

Instrument	Focus	Type	Admin. Time	Scoring	(1) Score Interpretation	(2) Reliability	(3) Validity	Availability
GENERAL ACROSS BUSINESS AND INDUSTRY (Continued)								
Styles of Leadership Survey (1986)	Leadership styles—Directive, supportive, bureaucratic, compromise, integrated	Self-report	?	Hand	Fair	Fair	Fair	Teleometrics International 1755 Woodstead Ct. The Woodlands, TX 77380
Styles of Management Inventory (1986)	Management style—Directive, supportive, bureaucratic, compromise, integrated	Self-report	?	Hand	Fair	Fair	Fair	Teleometrics International 1755 Woodstead Ct. The Woodlands, TX 77380
XYZ Inventory (1975)	Leadership style—Theory X, Y & Z	Self-report	20 minutes	Hand Machine	Fair	Poor-Fair	None	Organizational Tests, Ltd. Box 328 Fredericton, NB Canada
RESEARCH INSTRUMENTS								
Administrator Professional Leadership Scale (1974)	Principal Leadership effectiveness	Subordinate questionnaire	?	Hand	Fair	Not given	Fair	Bruce Thompson, *Refinement of Administrator Professional Leadership Scale* ERIC ED 175–911

Leadership Styles Instruments (Continued)

Instrument	Focus	Type	Admin. Time	Scoring	(1) Score Interpretation	(2) Reliability	(3) Validity	Availability
RESEARCH INSTRUMENTS (Continued)								
Humanistic Leadership Questionnaire (1981)	Principal leadership style—Humanism	Self-report Questionnaire	?	Hand	Fair	Not given	Not given	C. Eaglet and R. Cogdell. The Humanistic Leadership Model: A Pilot Investigation Ed Res. Quarterly, 5, 1981, 51–70
Instructional Activities Questionnaire (1984)	Principal	Teacher & principal functions	?	Hand	Fair	Not given	Fair	Terry Larsen University of Colorado Boulder CO
Leader Authenticity Scale (1982)	Principal authenticity	Subordinate questionnaire	?	Hand	Fair	Excellent	Good	James Henderson and Wayne Hoy Leader Authenticity: The development and test of an operational measure ERIC ED 219–408
Leadership/ Climate (1985)	Principal effectiveness	Subordinate questionnaire	?	Hand	Fair	Excellent	Fair	P. Watson, J. Crawford, and G. Kimball. The school makes a difference: Analysis of teacher perceptions of their principal and school climate. ERIC ED 266–529

SOURCE: Artr, Judith. *Assessing Leadership and Managerial Behavior* (1990), Northwest Regional Educational Laboratory, Portland, OR.

133

Bibliography

Aronowitz, S., & Giroux, H. A. (1993). *Education under siege* (2nd ed.). South Hadley, MA: Bergin and Garvey.

Bailey, G. D. (1990). *How to improve curriculum leadership: Twelve tenets. Tips for principals.* Reston, VA: National Association of Secondary School Principals.

Bandura, A. (1986). *Social foundations of thought and action: A social cognitive theory.* Englewood Cliffs, NJ: Prentice Hall.

Bandura, A. (1993). Perceived self-efficacy in cognitive development and functioning. *Educational Psychologist, 28*(2), 117–148.

Bandura, A. (1996). *Self-efficacy in changing societies.* New York: Cambridge University Press

Bandura, A. (1997). *Self-efficacy: The exercise of control.* New York: W. H. Freeman.

Barth, R. S. (1990). *Improving schools from within: Teachers, parents and principals can make the difference.* San Francisco: Jossey-Bass.

Bass, B. M. (1990). *Bass & Stodill's handbook of leadership: Theory, research and management application* (3rd ed.). New York: The Free Press.

Beck, L. G., & Murphy, J. (1993).*Understanding the principalship: Metaphorical themes 1920s–1990s.* New York: Teachers College Press.

Bennis, W. (1994). The 4 competencies of leadership. *Training and Development Journal, 38*(8), 15 19.

Bennis, W. (2003). *On becoming a leader* (3rd ed.). Cambridge, MA: Perseus Press.

Bennis, W. B., & Nanus, B. (1985). *Leaders: The strategies for taking charge.* New York: Harper & Row.

Blank, R. K. (1987). In what areas do principals provide school leadership? Evidence from a national sample of urban high schools. *ERS Spectrum, 5*(3), 24–33.

Bolman, L. G., & Deal, T. E. (2003). *Reframing organizations: Artistry, choice and leadership* (3rd ed.). San Francisco: Jossey-Bass.

Bonstingl, J. J. (2001). *Schools of quality* (3rd ed.). Thousand Oaks, CA: Corwin Press.

Carnegie Council on Adolescent Development. (1989). *Turning points: Preparing American youth for the 21st century.* Washington, DC: Author.

Conger, J. A. (1989). *The charismatic leader: Behind the mystique of exceptional leadership.* San Francisco: Jossey-Bass.

Conley, D. T., Goldman, P. (1994). *Ten propositions for facilitative leadership.* In J. Murphy & K. Seashore Louis (Eds.), *Reshaping the principalship: Insights from transformational reform efforts* (pp. 237–262). Newbury Park, CA: Corwin Press.

Council of Chief State School Officers. (1996). *Interstate School Leaders Licensure Consortium standards for school leaders.* Washington, DC: Author.

Council of the Great City Schools, U.S. Department of Education, & Institute for Educational Leadership. (1999, October). *Reaching consensus on urban education and improvement: A summary of 5 forums.* Washington, DC: U.S. Department of Education.

Curtis, M., & Stollar, S. (1996). Applying principles and practices of organizational change to school reform. *School Psychology Review, 25*(4), 409–417.

Daresh, J. C. (2006). Beginning the principalship: A practical guide for new school leaders (3rd ed.). Thousand Oaks, CA: Corwin Press.

Deal, T., & Peterson, K. (1998). *Shaping school culture: The heart of leadership.* San Francisco: Jossey-Bass.

Deans of School of Education at U.C. Berkeley, CSU Haywood, CSU San Francisco, and CSU San Jose. (1999, April 27). *Preparing leaders for urban schools: A vision for the millennium, a program for the present.* Unpublished paper.

Decker, L. E., et al. (1994). *Home-school-community relations: Trainers manual and study guide.* Charlottesville: University of Virginia, Mid-Atlantic Center for Community Education.

Educational Research Service, National Association of Elementary School Principals, & National Association of Secondary School Principals. (2000). *The principal, keystone of a high achieving school: Attracting and keeping the leaders we need.* Arlington, VA: ERS.

English, F. W. (1987). The principal as master architect of curricular unity. *NASSP Bulletin, 71*(498), 35–42.

English, F. W. (2000). *Deciding what to teach and test.* Thousand Oaks, CA: Corwin Press.

Epstein, J., Sanders, M. G., Simon, B. S., Clark Salinas, K., Rodriguez Jansorn, N., & Van Voorhis, F. L. (2002). *School, family, and community partnerships: Your handbook for action.* Thousand Oaks, CA: Corwin Press.

Evans, R. (1995, April 14). Getting real about leadership. *Education Week,* 29–36.

Evans, R. (1996). *The human side of school change.* San Francisco: Jossey-Bass.

Flora, C. B., & Flora, J. (1989). Characteristics of entrepreneurial communities in a time of crisis. *Rural Development News, 12*(2), 1–4.

Forsyth, P., & Tallerico, M. (1993). *City schools: Leading the way.* Thousand Oaks, CA: Corwin Press.

Fullan, M. (1993). *Change forces: Probing the depths of educational reform.* Bristol, PA: Falmer Press.

Fullan, M. (1998). Leadership for the 21st century: Breaking the bonds of dependency. *Educational Leadership, 55*(7), 6–10.

Gehrke, N. (1997). *In search of the better school curriculum. Working paper: Benchmarks for schools.* Washington, DC: U.S. Department of Education.

Glatthorn, A. A. (1994). *Developing a quality curriculum.* Alexandria, VA: Association for Supervision and Curriculum Development.

Goldman, P., Dunlap, D. & Conley, D. (1993). Facilitative power and nonstandardized solutions to school site restructuring. *Educational Administration Quarterly, 29*(1), 69–92.

Goldring, E. B., & Rallis, S. F. (2000). *Principals of dynamic schools* (2nd ed.). Thousand Oaks, CA: Corwin Press.

Grensing-Pophal, L. (1996). Seven communication traps and how you can avoid them. *Communication Briefings, 15*(6), 8a–8ab.

Hall, B. (1986). *The genesis effect: Personal and organizational transformations.* New York: Paulist Press.

Hall, G. E., & Loucks, S. F. (1978). Teacher concerns as a basis for facilitating staff development. *Teachers College Record, 80*(1).

Hutto, J. R., & Criss, G. D. (1996). Principal, finesse your way to instructional leadership. *Leader 123: Selected readings from the NASSP Bulletin.* Reston, VA: National Association of Secondary School Principals.

Jackson, G., & Costa, C. (1974). The inequality of educational opportunity in the Southwest: An observational study of ethnically mixed classrooms. *American Educational Research Journal, 11*(3), 219–229.

Jenkins, W. A., & Oliver, R. W. (1997). *The eagle and the monk.* Norwalk, CT: Gates and Bridges.

Johnson, J., Farkas, S., & Bers, A. (1997). *Getting by: What American teenagers really think about their schools.* New York: Public Agenda.

Johnson, S. (1998). *Who moved my cheese?* New York: G. P. Putnam's Sons.

Kohl, H. R. (1991). *I won't learn from you! The role of assent in learning.* Minneapolis, MN: Milkweed Editions.

Kouzes, J. M., & Posner, B. Z. (2002). *The leadership challenge* (3rd ed.). San Francisco: Jossey-Bass.

Lashway, L. (1997). *Visionary leadership.* Eugene: University of Oregon. (ERIC Document Reproduction Service No. ED 402 643)

Levine, J. A., Murphy, D. & Wilson, S. D. (1993). *Getting men involved: Strategies for early childhood programs.* New York: Scholastic.

Lewis, A. (1993). *Leadership styles.* Arlington, VA: American Association of School Administrators.

Lindley, F. A. (2003). *The portable mentor: A resource guide for entry-year principals and mentors.* Thousand Oaks, CA: Corwin Press.

MacGregor Burns, J. (1982). *Leadership.* New York: Harper Perennial.

Marzano, R. J., Waters, T., & McNulty, B. A. (2005). *School leadership that works.* Alexandria, VA & Aurora, CO: Association for Supervision and Curriculum Development.

The Master Teacher. (1991). *Learning a lesson from towns that are growing.* Manhattan, KS: Author.

McColl, A. (2005, April). Tough call: Is No Child Left Behind constitutional? *Phi Delta Kappan,* 604–610.

McEwan, E. K. (2003). *10 traits of highly effective principals.* Thousand Oaks, CA: Corwin Press.

Michalko, M. (1998, May). Thinking like a genius. *The Futurist,* 21–25.

Miller, J. P. (2000). *Education and the soul.* Albany: State University of New York Press.

Moles, O. C. (1996). *Reaching all families: Creating family-friendly schools.* Washington DC: United States Department of Education, Office of Educational Research and Improvement.

Nanus, B. (1994, Summer). Questions of leadership. *USC Business,* 44–49.

National Association of Elementary School Principals. (1996). *Standards for quality elementary and middle schools, kindergarten through eighth grade* (3rd ed.). Alexandria, VA: Author.

National Association of Secondary School Principals. (1996). *Breaking ranks: Changing an American institution.* Reston, VA: Author.

National Committee for Citizens in Education. (1993) *Taking stock* [pamphlet]. Washington, DC. 1993: Author.

Northwest Regional Educational Laboratory. (n.d.). *Partnerships by design: Cultivating effective meaningful school-family-community partnerships.* Retrieved May 15, 2006, from www.nwrel.org/partnerships

Novak, J. M. (2005). Invitational leadership. In B. Davies (Ed.), *The essentials of school leadership* (pp. 44–60). London & Thousand Oaks, CA: Paul Chapman Publishing and Corwin Press.

Payne, R. (1998, Fall). Speaking their language: Working with students and adults from poverty. *Infocus: NASSP, 2*(1), 6.

Peters, T. (1988). *Thriving on chaos.* Reading, MA: Addison-Wesley.

Peters, T., & Austin, N. (1985). *A passion for excellence: The leadership difference.* New York: Random House.

Peters, T. J., & Waterman, R., Jr. (2004). *In search of excellence.* New York: Harper-Business Essentials.

Polite, V. C., McClure, R., & Rollie, D. L. (1997). The emerging reflective urban principal: The role of shadowing encounters. *Urban Education, 31*(5), 466–489.

Public Agenda. (1997). *Getting by: What American teenagers really think about their schools.* New York: Author.

Purkey, W. W. (1996). *Inviting school success* (3rd ed.). Belmont, CA: Wadsworth.

Purkey, W., & Novak, J. (1978). *Inviting school success: A self-concept approach to teaching and learning* (2nd ed.). Belmont, CA: Wadsworth.

Quality counts: The urban challenge report. (1998, January 8). *Education Week, 17*(17), 1–270.

Saphier, J., & King, M. (1985). Good seeds grown in strong cultures. *Educational Leadership, 42*(6), 67–74.

Seashore Louis, K., & Miles, M. B. (1990). *Improving the urban high school: What works and why.* New York & London: Teachers College Press.

Schein, E. H. (1999). Empowerment, coercive persuasion and organizational learning: Do they connect? *Learning Organization, 6*(4), 163–172.

Schwahn, C. J., & Spady, W. G. (1998). *Total leaders: Applying the best future-focused change strategies to education.* Arlington, VA: The American Association of School Administrators.

Secretan, L. J. K. (1996). *Reclaiming higher ground: Creating organizations that inspire soul.* Toronto: Macmillan Canada.

Sergiovanni, T. J. (1990a). Advances in leadership theory and practice. *Advances in educational administration* (Vol. 1, pp. 10–19). Greenwich, CT: JAI Press.

Sergiovanni, T. J. (1990b). *Value added leadership: How to get extraordinary performance in schools.* San Diego, CA: Harcourt Brace Jovanovich.

Simpson, A. W., & Erickson, M. T. (1983). Teachers' verbal and nonverbal communication patterns as a function of teacher race, student gender and student race. *American Educational Research Journal, 20*(2), 183–198.

Smith, S. C., & Piele, P. K. (2006). *School leadership handbook for excellence* (4th ed.). Thousand Oaks, CA: Corwin Press.

Smith, W. F., & Andrews, R. L. (1989). *Instructional leadership: How principals make a difference.* Alexandria, VA: Association for Supervision and Curriculum Development.

Standerfer, L. (2005). Subgroups are not just testing groups. *Newsleader, 53*(4), 4.

Strong, J. H. (1993, May). Defining the principalship: Instructional leader as middle manager. *NASSP Bulletin,* 1–7.

Tschannen-Moran, M., Woolfolk Hoy, A. & Hoy, W. K. (1998). Teacher efficacy: Its meaning and measure. *Review of Educational Research, 68*(2), 202–248.

Weiner, L. (1993). *Preparing teachers for urban schools.* New York: Teachers College Press.

Wilkins, W. (1999a). Take risks when there's no danger. *The Futurist, 33*(5), 60.

Wilkins, W. (1999b, August). *Taking risks to engage your personal frontiers.* Unpublished paper presented at the World Future Society Annual Conference, Washington, DC.

Yin, R. K., & White, J. L. (1986). *Managing for excellence in urban high schools: District and school roles. Final report.* Washington, DC: U.S. Department of Education. (ERIC Document Reproduction Service No. ED318837)

Yukl, G. A. (1989). *Leadership in organizations.* Englewood Cliffs, NJ: Prentice Hall.

Index

CORWIN PRESS

The Corwin Press logo—a raven striding across an open book—represents the union of courage and learning. Corwin Press is committed to improving education for all learners by publishing books and other professional development resources for those serving the field of PreK–12 education. By providing practical, hands-on materials, Corwin Press continues to carry out the promise of its motto: **"Helping Educators Do Their Work Better."**